No Enemy of Mine

No Enemy of Mine

TERRI POTTS
From interviews with
GERDA MCMILLAN

VANCOUVER, WASHINGTON

Copyright © 2014 by Terri Potts
All Rights Reserved

First Edition

Photo credits: pages 1, 3, 51, and 135 were found on Wikipedia and are free for use in the public domain; author's photo by Valorie Webster; all other images are from the photo collection of Gerda McMillan, used with her express permission.

Cover design and book layout by Montage BioGraphics
www.montagebiographics.com

ISBN-13: 978-0692278185

Printed in the United States of America

This book is dedicated with love and admiration to Gerda McMillan. She has never let anything get her down, always facing life head-on with courage, optimism and, above all, enthusiasm!

During the course of working with Gerda, she has not only become my good friend, she is also one of those people in my life I refer to as "the family we choose".

— *Terri Potts*

CHAPTER ONE

MY STORY READS like a Grimm fairy tale. The original versions, you know, were not all sweetness and light. They often taught the unfortunate realities of life, which I guess is what a good fairy tale should do. They should, because the real world can be a terrible awakening for over-protected children with unrealistic expectations in life.

While many fairy tales begin with a beautiful princess living in a fabulous castle, mine begins in a modest cottage in the tiny *dorf* (village) of Oberkassel, in the *Rhein* (Rhine) Valley of Germany. It was the summer of 1924 — July 16th — in the lull between the storms of World War I and World War II. A midwife delivered me. It was common practice.

I was a slim child with blond hair and eyes that were sometimes blue and often green.

Oberkassel was, at that time, a tiny gem among many that studded the broad, fertile belt of the *Rhein* Valley. It was situated at the northern extent of the

Siebengebirge (Seven Mountains), a range of more than forty heavily wooded hills and mountains so named, perhaps, because it is said that from any given viewpoint one can never see more than seven at a time.

What a magical place it was—the land of fairy tales and dragons! Siegfried, the hero of legend, slew the mighty dragon Fafnir in his lair at *Drachenfels* (Dragon's Rock), just seven miles from my home. In fact, many legends and fairy tales have their roots in the *Siebengebirge*. Stories like "Cinderella", "Rapunzel" and "Snow White and the Seven Dwarfs". Those dwarfs worked in the rock quarries of the *Siebengebirge*, just as my father did, when I was a child.

My father, Josef Velten (ca. 1896 – 1960), was an intelligent, happy-go-lucky person. He came from a large family, with eight siblings. Like most families in the area, they grew produce for sale in the city of Bonn, on the west bank of the *Rhein*.

Bonn was accessible to us by bridge from nearby Beuel, on the east bank. This bridge was built in the late 1800's, when the people of Bonn finally gave up on getting any help from uncooperative Beuel and decided to build a bridge by themselves. They saw the value of facilitating commerce between the two, but the people of Beuel were not so sure, especially the ferrymen, who worried it would put them out of business.

It was a beautiful bridge. On either end were twin, castle-like towers joined by stone archways. When it was complete, one final touch was added: the statue of a boy (*Brückenmännchen*), bending over to

Chapter One

Artist's rendering of the Bonn-Rheinebrucke

Brückenmännchen

point his little bottom contemptuously at Beuel. The message was clear: "Here, that's what we think of you, not wanting to help us!"

This similarity with the situation between Vancouver, Washington and Portland, Oregon, in which they cannot agree on the building of a much-needed bridge, is not lost on me. In fact, it makes me realize that, although I am far from my home in Oberkassel, people everywhere share the same concerns and operate in pretty much the same way. There is a certain comfort to be found in that.

There are many small villages along the *Rhein*, and the hills are dotted with castles and castle ruins. Like MAX here, in the Portland metropolitan area, trains connect one town to another, and there was a station right next to the little house where we went to live with my grandparents, shortly after I was born. It was a white stucco house with ivy growing up the walls.

I loved being there! I would go into the fields and pick flowers to make little bouquets. When the train stopped on its way to Römlinghoven, the resort town next to ours, I would be at the station with my flowers in a basket, and I sold them. I was the flower girl.

I used to babysit for a couple that had a nursery, where they grew flowers and vegetables. In the summer, I would take their little children up into the hills. In the hot afternoons we walked through the fields down to the river and went swimming in the *Rhein*.

My older sister and I had to walk to school, and on the way we would pass this one house I particularly remember. I used to go visit in that house,

Chapter One

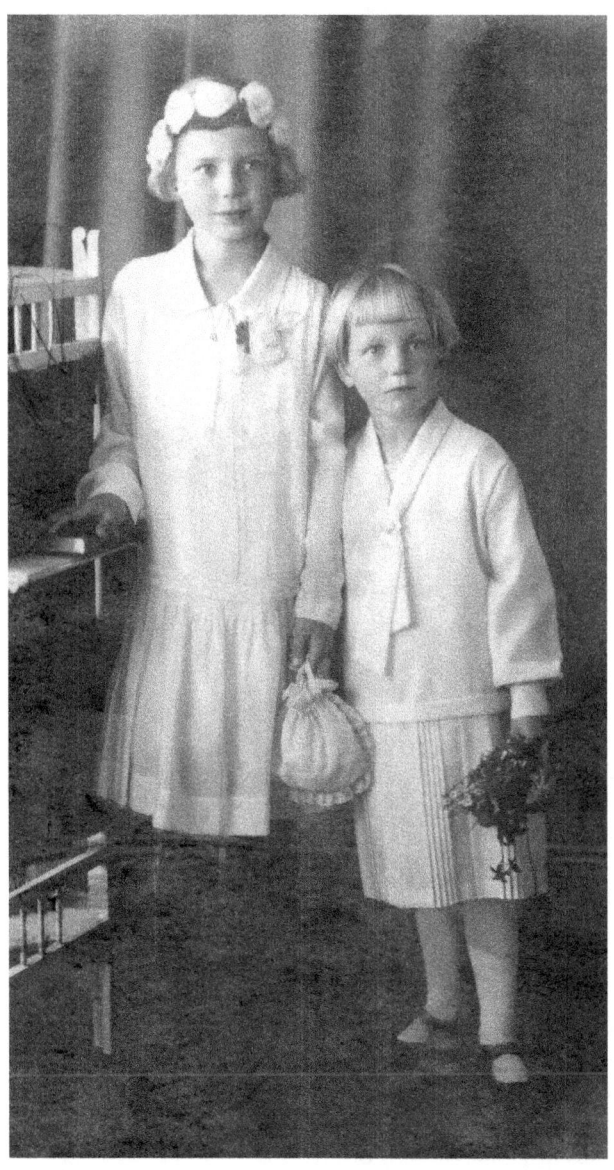

ca. 1931 Christina (Christel) and Gertrud (Gerda) Velten

because they had a piano and they let me play on it. I loved music! My mother took me, one time, to see if I had any qualification, but right there they told my mother, "No, she doesn't." I tell you, in Germany, if you are not real good, you are turned down very quickly. Nevertheless, in the ensuing years I did a pretty fair job with the harmonica and the accordion, playing one or both nearly every day, just for the simple pleasure of it.

We didn't have very much, at the time, and the people who owned the piano were well-to-do. Their children had everything—so in the winter, when it snowed, I would borrow their little sled and fly down one of the nearby hills.

I was deadly afraid of their dog, because I was always afraid he would come snapping at my heels when I ran to school. This was a fear passed down to me from my mother.

She was terribly afraid of anything with four legs and always said, "If it crawls, step on it!" Maybe this was because she was a city girl, born and raised in *Köln* (Cologne).

Her parents were Christian and Christina Lennartz. In addition to my mother, they had nine other children. One of the boys was my mother's twin, Rudolf, but I never knew much about any of the other siblings.

Elisabeth "Lisa" Lennartz—my mother—met my father when he went to *Köln* as a young man to work in a Schnapps distillery. It can only have been true love that brought her with him to our little village. I don't remember my mother and father as

Chapter One

Elisabeth (Lennartz) Velten ca. 1914

being terribly demonstrative with one another, but I know — just because I know — that they were very much in love and content with their lives, in spite of whatever struggles they faced together.

In those early years, I was not aware of the economic challenges of the times, that Germany was being crushed beneath the weight of its war reparation debt to France and England; that unemployment was high and foreign trade was hampered by tariffs levied against German products around the world. I was not aware of it when the treasury began printing too much money, which led to inflation and a worthless German mark. The price of everything skyrocketed; even the bare essentials were beyond the reach of many people. With the advent of The Great Depression, U.S. investment capital dried up and loans were called in.

In 1931, they closed the quarry at Stenzelberg, where my father worked. It was the last of the quarries that had been in operation in the *Siebengebirge* for centuries. The stones from those quarries were used to build castles and cathedrals as far back as the twelfth century. With the closing of the quarry, my father turned his efforts to selling produce.

When I was nine, my father moved our family across the *Rhein*, into the heart of Bonn.

Our new home was in an apartment above a candy store. I was so sad to leave Oberkassel! I missed my friends. I missed the hills. But this move would save him the daily trip back and forth to the *versteigerung* (wholesale produce market), which was

CHAPTER ONE

located in Bonn *Markthalle*, just two or three blocks from our new home.

1935 Joseph, Gerda and Elisabeth Velten at the markthalle

Each morning, my father would go to this place where all the sellers came to offer their produce. It was set up with bleachers lining a drive where the sellers would bring their horse-drawn wagons filled with produce. There was a reader-board, and as each took their turn, upon it would appear what they had to offer. Buyers would sit in the bleachers, and each seat was fitted with a button you would push. Father's number was seventy-one. If he decided he wanted what they were selling, he would push the button and his number would appear on the board, telling them he wanted to buy the produce. Then he would pay the clerk and, like all the other buyers, have the produce delivered to his little wooden structure in the *markthalle* where he ran his business.

My routine was to get up every morning, dress for school and go to the *markthalle*. For breakfast, I went to the cantina there, where I bought liver sausage and *brötchen* (hard rolls). Oh, I loved the liver sausage and *brötchen*! In the winter, when father sold Christmas trees in the square at *Beethovenplatz* (Beethoven Plaza), I would deliver them, and often the customers would give me a tip for my trouble. Then I would run across the square to buy a cup of hot chocolate from a nearby vendor. I remember fondly there was a man there roasting chestnuts.

Bonn was a beautiful city; very modern, with a well-respected university, lovely museums, parks and statues; there were old cemeteries, where many famous people were buried; Beethoven was born in Bonn — his family home is now a museum. But, when I first moved there, most of this was lost on me. It wasn't until later that I truly came to appreciate the city.

Going to school in Bonn was very unpleasant for me, at first. Having come from a country school, I was a bit behind the other students. This left me feeling isolated and alone. It was difficult to make new friends, but I did, eventually, become good friends with a little girl in my neighborhood. Her last name was Birnbaum, which means "pear tree".

My mother helped with the produce stand, so after the work day was done our family would go to the deli for dinner. On weekends, if the weather was good, we would have dinner at Im Bären, our favorite restaurant in Bonn, and then we would buy ice cream cones and go for a walk along the *Rhein*.

CHAPTER ONE

Just before Lent it was traditional to have a carnival — we called it *Fastnacht*. It was like Mardi Gras. People went crazy in the streets and there were parades with colorful floats, many of them poking irreverent fun at government officials. Candy was thrown to the throng along the parade route. And there was always a stage set up somewhere where anyone could get up in front of a crowd. My mother, a true daughter of *Köln*, which was notorious for its humor, would jump up on the stage and perform comedy. My sister and I thought it was so embarrassing!

By this time, the economy in Germany — now fully under Hitler's control since the death of President Hindenburg in 1934 — appeared to have improved greatly. He had started a big public works program, while at the same time establishing price controls. There was almost no unemployment.

In the good times in Germany it was just like here: you could go shopping and have beautiful things, although in Germany everything was quality. In America, people want quantity — the more the better — but Germans are for quality. And that's me: I'd rather have less, as long as what I have is good. To quote Oscar Wilde, "The best is good enough for me!" I have always liked this saying, because I feel the same. Why spend your money for nothing? If you have a champagne appetite and a beer budget, then you buy fewer things, but that doesn't mean you can't have quality.

Chapter Two

At ten years old, I was sent to live for six weeks with "foster parents" in northern Bavaria, near the *Mangfallbrücke* (Mangfall Bridge) — one of the highest bridges in Germany, which was then under construction as part of the autobahn project. Hitler, who had been appointed Chancellor that year, strongly supported the philosophy of *blut und boden* (blood and soil), believing the strength of the German people came from their long history of working the land. Children from the cities were sent out to farms to get fresh air and experience rural life.

Oh, that was quite an experience! It was an all-day trip by train from Bonn to our first stop in southeastern Bavaria, where we began making several stops to deliver children. Finally, we came to the village where I and three or four other children got off. It was less than ninety miles from where Hitler was born, in Braunau am Inn, which is just barely across the border into Austria.

Chapter Two

We had on our name tags with the names of our foster parents. When mine spotted me, they said, "Oh, you are Gertrud. You come with us."

They had a big farmhouse and ten cows. I was afraid of the cows, of course, afraid of anything that walked on four legs, but I was delighted by the muscial sound of the cowbells they wore around their necks.

Here, I had to sleep in a room upstairs by myself. At home, I was accustomed to sleeping in a room with my sister, Christel. There was a huge, huge tree right by my window, and we had a thunder storm that first night. I thought it was going to strike the tree and burn down the house! Oh, I was so scared! So then, lucky me, there was another girl who had also been on the train. She was staying in another foster home, and she, too, was afraid. So they put us together, and that helped.

One of the stories we heard as children was about witches. There was, of course, a barn on the family's property, and the other little girl and I were curious to see what was inside. All of the accoutrements of farming were there, as well as something that was probably a scale for weighing things, but it looked like a big, wide swing. We were looking at it when we heard a shuffling sound. Here came this old crone of a woman, creeping along. We thought she was a witch! We tore out of the barn and never went in there again. I have no idea what she was doing there, but we didn't wait to find out!

During the week, I barely ate anything at all because I didn't like the food. They often served *leber klöse* (liver dumplings). Ugh! But on weekends, I ate with great enthusiasm, because they served fish!

Our foster family had a hired man, named Zepple. At night, after the cows were all milked, Zepple had to go to the dairy, and he took us with him. They had this fabulous treat, like a little cake, or pretzel. So we loved going with Zepple!

The school kids from that little town invited us to go on a trip to beautiful Lake Chiemsee, in southern Bavaria. There were two major islands on the lake: *Herreninsel* (Men's Island) and *Fraueninsel* (Women's Island). We were to visit the beautiful castle on *Herreninsel*, but the only way to get there was by boat. It was frightening, because whenever the little boat rose on a swell it seemed like it was going to come right up out of the water! When we got there, before we could go inside, we were told to take off our shoes. In our stockings we just slid through there like we were skating on ice. The floors were almost like a mirror. King Ludwig II started construction on the castle in 1878. It was intended to be largely the same as the palace at Versailles, in tribute to King Louis IV of France, whom he admired, but Ludwig halted construction in 1885. The north wing was never fully completed, so it was demolished, but what remains is quite impressive.

౧

Little did any of us know the good times in Germany would come at a terrible price. Beneath the surface, there was a growing crisis. Hitler's economic measures, which included a large military build-up, were leading to a huge national debt.

In August of 1936, in response to this crisis, Hitler wrote the "Four-Year Plan Memorandum". In it, he warned of an imminent, cataclysmic struggle between Judeo-Bolshevism and German National Socialism, which would threaten the very survival of Germany.

Here is an excerpt from that memo:

> *Since the outbreak of the French Revolution, the world has been moving with ever increasing speed toward a new conflict, the most extreme solution of which is called Bolshevism, whose essence and aim, however, are solely the elimination of those strata of mankind which have hitherto provided the leadership and their replacement by worldwide Jewry. No state will be able to withdraw or even remain at a distance from this historical conflict... It is not the aim of this memorandum to prophesy the time when the untenable situation in Europe will become an open crisis. I only want, in these lines, to set down my conviction that this crisis cannot and will not fail to arrive and that it is Germany's duty to secure her own existence by every means in face of this catastrophe, and to protect herself against it, and that from this compulsion there arises a series of conclusions relating to the most important tasks that our people have ever been set. For*

> *a victory of Bolshevism over Germany would not lead to a Versailles treaty, but to the final destruction, indeed the annihilation of the German people...I consider it necessary for the Reichstag to pass the following two laws: 1) A law providing the death penalty for economic sabotage and 2) A law making the whole of Jewry liable for all damage inflicted by individual specimens of this community of criminals upon the German economy, and thus upon the German people.*

In retrospect, his words were a pretty clear declaration of his intent. But, as far as I — a young, twelve-year-old girl — knew, things were good. I was pretty carefree.

Then, one day in 1937, they came to find me. As usual, I was roller skating — I skated everywhere I went. They told me I needed to go to the hospital to see my mother. I already knew she was sick. She'd gone out one evening to find my father, who hadn't come home for supper. I don't remember if she was worried or angry, but she found him at a *wirtshaus* (tavern). As a result of wandering around in the cool night air, she caught a cold. It lingered, but none of us realized it was becoming something worse, until finally she had to be hospitalized, and we learned she had double pneumonia. They gave her morphine, which made her quite delirious, and even though that was frightening to me, I believed she would be okay, now that she was in the doctor's care.

Chapter Two

Now, when I got to the hospital, one of the nuns — most hospitals were run by nuns — came and said, "I'll take you downstairs."

"*Nein, nein!*" I cried. "I don't want to go down there!" I knew it could only mean one thing, because that was where all the dead people were. I simply could not do it.

It was hard to believe she was gone — that lively woman who so embarrassed me when she got up on stage during *Fastnacht*. At that moment, I would have given anything to see her do it again.

There is a deep ache in my heart that will never go away: I didn't get to say "good-bye" to her.

She was only forty-three years old!

It was the tradition to wear black for one year. All black. I can hardly stand to wear black now.

After she died — oh, this was a horrible time! My sister, Christel, was four years older than I, which would make her seventeen at the time. We only had a two-bedroom apartment, so we slept in the same room. After my mother died, my father started drinking heavily. One day, Christel and I were in our bedroom. My nose twitched.

"Christel, I smell something!"

It was a lucky thing I have such a sensitive nose — oh, I can smell anything. We ran to investigate. Dad was slouched in a chair in the kitchen. He was drunk! In the kitchen we discovered he had turned on the gas — without lighting it! It was intentional; he wanted to get rid of us all!

"Dad!" we yelled. And it was like he was coming out of a trance. We were scared; oh, we were scared.

You can imagine how hard it would have been to get any sleep after that!

Father remarried very quickly. One of the men at the *versteigerung* told his daughter, who was currently raising one son by herself, about this successful man at the market who had just lost his wife. She wasted no time going after him. And she got him!

He moved us all to a different apartment. It was in a building behind a large beverage-distribution center, above a repair shop on Viktoriastraße. We had to come through a big door to get into that back building where we were living. The repair shop was on the *primären* (main floor; primary level). It was owned by a blacksmith. He was a bachelor, who kept very much to himself. A fellow with his wife and two children lived on the first floor above; we lived above that, on the second floor. I remember there was a little boy in the neighborhood, too. One day, he cornered me on the stairs in my building and tried to kiss me. I was disgusted and pushed him away.

Our apartment was right next door to a kindergarten. I would hang on the fence, watching the kids play, and the nuns were in charge. The nuns were always in charge. It was Catholic. I made up my mind right there that I wanted to become a kindergarten teacher.

The *Marienshule* (St. Mary's Catholic grade school) I went to was just a block away and the *markthalle* about two blocks — three blocks at the most — so it was all in that area. Again, I would roller skate everywhere I went. I wore the kind of skates you just strap on and go.

Chapter Two

Father still drank heavily — not all the time, but when he did, he'd often go on binges for days at a time. When he wasn't drinking, from time to time he'd take me up to the old quarry with him, where he had a small parcel of land he cultivated to grow vegetables. And sometimes he'd take me to a soccer game. We both reveled in the raw energy of the crowd, forgetting our troubles for a while as we got swept up in the action on the field. Those are precious memories for me.

But those times were few and far between.

Christel was gone much of the time, because she was working, and I had to put up with my stepmother by myself. I did not like her! I know, now, that she lacked maturity and wisdom, but when she immediately insisted that Christel and I call her "Mom", she destroyed any chance that I would see her in that role. In fact, I couldn't even call her by name. All that came out was just, "Hey!" I was angry, unhappy and felt very alone. I was just thirteen! — at the age when girls need their mothers most, to teach them things, to offer advice. But I could not, and would not, accept her as my mother.

My father's parents, Adam and Gertrud Velten, had nine children. When they died they left the house to their oldest son, which was the custom. My *Onkel* (Uncle) Adam and his wife (also Gertrud) sold it and bought the little house where I was born, and now their son, my cousin Ulrich, still owns that house. After we moved to Bonn, whenever we went by the *Rhein* and the little ferry boat came, I would drive my mother crazy.

"Give me money! Let me go to Oberkassel!"

And she would finally give in exclaiming, "Here's the money. Just go!"

And then, where would I go? — to my uncle and aunt. After my mother died, they knew how sad I was, and they were very nice to me. But, at the end of the day, I would always have to return to that apartment, where my stepmother lived, where my father was no longer really there for me.

My home life was so miserable, even the nearby orphanage looked more appealing to me. Whenever I walked by it I would think, I wish I could live there. I saw that their lives were regimented, unlike mine, and they appeared to be well cared for.

I started babysitting the children on the first floor of our apartment building. Their father — let's call him *Herr* Müller (although that isn't really his name) — drove a delivery truck for a major worldwide beverage company. He was handsome and probably twenty years older than me. I had a huge crush on him. I couldn't really see then that he had an eye for the ladies. In fact, he tried to get close to my sister, but she had another friend, see, so she told him, "Get lost!" Then he looked in my direction. I can see that, now, but then I just loved him tremendously, because I was a young girl. I thought, Oh! He doesn't like his wife. He likes me! I was flattered by his attention.

He was quite willing to take advantage of my admiration. After dancing into the wee hours of the morning, he and his wife would arrive home to find the children in bed and I, too, would be asleep in

CHAPTER TWO

the parents' bed. Rather than waking me up to send me home, they would crawl into bed, as well, and he always made sure he was next to me. I would wake up to the feel of his hand on my body. I held my breath and pretended I was still asleep. It was very confusing. He was like a father figure, but he was also a man, and I was just a naïve young girl, too scared to make a sound.

One day, *Herr* Müller asked me, "Gerda" — he was the first to call me that, instead of Gertrud, which was my true, given name — "would you like to go with me on my deliveries?"

I jumped at the chance and talked my sister into writing a note, excusing me from school. Oh, I was so excited! We drove out into the country, and he made his deliveries. One of those deliveries was to a little country inn in the nearby village of Kardorf. I'm sure he had some less than honorable intentions in mind, but I was oblivious; it was just a wonderful day. I loved that little country inn!

Several days later, when I was helping to bag groceries at the little store in our neighborhood, *Herr* Müller came by. He leaned down and whispered in my ear that he had left something for me in the restroom. It was a pair of nylon stockings, with the seam up the back! It was an outrageously inappropriate gift for him to give me, but I didn't think that at the time. It was a lovely secret and made me feel very grown up.

Chapter Three

IN RETROSPECT, THE first ominous sign of the coming war was when they began constructing the stark concrete buildings that would serve as air raid shelters. Several of them were built in Bonn. At the time, I didn't know what they were, but I did notice them. Obviously, Hitler was making preparations.

On a cold morning in November of 1938, I saw on my walk to school that the windows had been broken out of many of the buildings along the way. I had no idea what all had happened during that night, but later I learned that throughout Germany mobs of people had attacked Jewish people in the streets, broken into their homes and businesses and burned more than a thousand synagogues. More than ninety Jews were killed and hundreds more were injured. Seven thousand businesses were destroyed or damaged. This horrific night would later become known as *die Kristallnacht* (the Crystal Night), the "night of broken glass", which seems far too elegant a name to describe such mindless terrorizing and brutality.

When I got to school, I saw that my best friend — whom I just loved — wasn't there. I never saw her again. Her family was Jewish, which of course I didn't even know — they are Jewish and we are this — that just never entered our minds as children. On that day, thirty thousand Jews were arrested and sent to concentration camps. It was terrible! But I didn't learn this until much later, after the war was over. All I knew, then, was that my best friend was gone, without a word to explain what had happened to her.

Here, in America, I once overheard someone say, "I never met a German yet who knew anything about what they were doing to the Jews."

A couple of years after the war, a friend of mine told me that even though they lived near one of the concentration camps, they never knew what was going on there. They would see people coming and going, but if you questioned what was happening, they would get rid of you!

Obviously there were many Germans — those directly involved with those horrific, inhuman atrocities — who knew very well what was going on. Most people knew the Jews were being singled out and persecuted, but I knew nothing of what was going on inside those camps, and I'm convinced there were many, many people who did not know. Even in America, it is sometimes difficult to know the truth of what the government is doing; you can imagine how much more difficult it would be in a country where the regime is totalitarian, information is jealously guarded, and opposition is brutally dealt with.

The German people as a whole, whether guilty or innocent, have been paying for the deeds of the Nazis and those who followed their orders. They will, collectively, always bear the stain, but it is fair to understand that a lot of good people have suffered along with the bad.

ෆ

In 1937, a law had been passed that all women under twenty-five must do a *pflichtjahr* (compulsory year) — one year of domestic work. The Nazi party, and especially Hitler, believed women were to be good wives and mothers and, in this way, serve the *Reich*. So when I finished two years of school in home economics after grade-school, I lived at home and went every day for one year on my bike to work for this family. I was fourteen.

They were wonderful people and lived in a big, beautiful home. He was a professor. The professor and his wife had ten children. Each morning, when I arrived, there were ten little pairs of shoes for me to polish.

That was my first job. And I have lovely memories from the year I was there. On Easter we took the children to the park to hunt for colorful Easter eggs. At Christmas the high ceilings in their home allowed for a large, lovely tree, which they decorated beautifully. The children had to go to bed early on Christmas Eve, and in the morning I came to work again, so I

Chapter Three

saw their joy as they found their gifts beneath the tree. It was quite a wonderful experience that year. For the first time I learned what a family could be like; what it was like to live in a nice home and have beautiful things.

That was also the year I came down with scarlet fever. I don't remember much about it, except that I ran a very high fever and had a terribly sore throat. I was still in the hospital when my father was drafted. He wasn't going to be a soldier, but they were recruiting men for other duties. They were sending him to Kassel. He came to the hospital with my sister to see me, but we had to say our good-byes from opposite sides of a glass partition. Christel eventually caught the fever, too.

By the time my *pflichtjahr* came to an end, the contrast at home was more unbearable than ever. I was now fifteen and even more inclined to clash with my stepmother. The fact that my father was away a lot of the time made things even worse.

She told me I needed to find a paying job, so I started looking around. Then one day I came home to find my belongings had been packed in a bag and left outside on the landing. When I tried to open the door, I found it was locked.

"Please, let me in!" I yelled.

But my stepmother stood on the other side and said harshly, "Go away! Your father and I don't want you anymore."

I don't think my father ever knew what she said. Although he was often distracted, my father and I had a good relationship. He loved me and always treated me well. Some of my favorite memories are of times when we walked together along the *Rhein* — he pushing his bicycle and me walking along beside him.

At the time, though, her words dealt me a devastating blow! I had no money and nowhere to go.

Then it came to me — that little country inn!

Fortunately for me, the owner, Frau Esser, was looking for help. She gave me room and board and paid me a modest wage. I enjoyed my new job and the freedom it offered. My duties were to help out in the kitchen, run errands by train to nearby villages, clean the rooms and make up the beds; sometimes I worked behind the bar in the restaurant.

If it was in my mind that the relationship with *Herr* Müller would flower and bloom, I was greatly disappointed. I didn't see him much after I moved to Kardorf — just when he made his deliveries.

But, I had plenty of boyfriends, and on May Day there was a tree on my roof, as was the tradition — young men would put them up to signify their interest, usually anonymously. There was one young man, in particular. We used to walk into the hills and pick strawberries and cherries, because they just grew wild. Sometimes he came and asked me to go to the next town on our bikes. I really liked him. If things had gone differently, I might have been *Frau* Heck.

In those days, I had lots of fun. On my days off, I sometimes hung out with my cousin, *Onkel* Adam's daughter, also named Gertrud. She was something! We'd go swimming at a place called the Strand *Bad* (baths) and then we'd lay there sunning ourselves.

CHAPTER THREE

Suddenly, I'd notice that she was gone! I'd look out at the river and there she'd be, swimming out to one of the *schleppers* — that's what we called them in "low German" — those barges that hauled things downriver from Holland to Switzerland. She'd hop a ride! I was amazed at her audacity!

1944 Gerda and Gertrud at Strand Bad

After swimming, we would clean up and go somewhere for a nice dinner. Then we would go dancing. Dancing was the main entertainment available to us.

We missed the last train back from another village, after one such evening. A soldier offered to walk us home. The walk would be several miles, and it was way out of his way, but he was interested in me, and I led him to believe we would go out. Poor boy! I was young and fickle. Several days later, he turned up at the inn at what I guess was the appointed hour, but I wasn't there. I had completely forgotten! I was out dancing! You see, even as Hitler was invading Poland, the imperatives of youth still prevailed.

During this period of freedom and discovery in my own life, things were really beginning to change in Germany. Hitler's plans were coming to fruition. His focus on the youth of Germany — particularly young men — was producing a well of unquestioning devotion from which he could draw. Germany's youth were the nation's hope; they were the strength and the future of Germany! Every thought, every act was for Germany and for the Führer. These messages were drilled into their heads from the time they were ten years old.

My stepbrother, Willy, was recruited into the German army. He was a brilliant young man — broad-shouldered and tall — who, before the war, had been studying to become a foreign journalist. He spoke seven languages fluently, so he rose quickly within the ranks. At home we spoke what is known as "low" German. When we were at school, or if you would go to the doctor or talk to people you didn't know, you would speak "high" German. Willy, with his love of language, made a tape for me once describing things in "low"

CHAPTER THREE

German. It was hilarious because it sounded so ridiculous!

Father was not at all political. He never spoke about politics. His brother, my *Onkel* Adam, was quite gung-ho about Hitler. As things progressed, whenever we got up to leave at the end of a visit with him, instead of saying "*Gute nacht!*" we would have to say "*Heil Hitler! Sieg heil!*"

ca. 1939 Gerda, Josef and wife, cousin Ulrich, Onkel Adam, Tante Gertrud, cousin Teresa

My *Onkel* Sebastian, Father's youngest brother, was drafted into the *Schutzstaffel* (the SS). They were the German military elite. He was fortunate, in that he was a skilled tailor. They put him to good use making uniforms, but he never saw any action. I always admired his wife — *Tante* (Aunt) Änne. I liked everything she did. She had exquisite taste, always dressed very fashionably and never seemed to question the cost of anything she bought. Her father was high up in the Army, I think, and she was an only child, so she didn't want for anything.

Onkel Heinrich made the mistake of speaking his mind about Hitler one night at a restaurant. Any real or imagined opponent of the Nazi regime could be arrested without a specific reason and detained indefinitely. There was no trial, no opportunity to defend himself; *Onkel* Hein was dragged off to do hard labor in one of the Emsland camps, on the moors of northern Germany — probably Börgermoor, Esterwegen or Neusustrum. These were not Jewish concentration camps. They were for political prisoners, dissidents and other criminals. It was Hitler's goal to cultivate about 124,000 acres of the moors and settle the area with farmers. Prisoners in those camps provided a labor pool and were treated horrifically. They were given only manual tools to perform back-breaking tasks. The guards regularly abused their charges. It is doubtful Uncle Hein made it out alive. I never heard anything more about him.

Onkel Ferdinand was married, with two children. He was never in the military, to my knowledge.

As the war intensified and grew broader in scope, its influence became more and more a part of our everyday lives. Work was hard, food was getting scarce and everything was expensive, because so much of the country's resources were going into the war effort.

It was common to greet someone you knew on the street with, "*Wie geths*?" (How are you?)

And the response would be, "*Man lebt.*" (One lives.)

Chapter Three

There was a song that became very popular during the war — "Lili Marleen". The song came from a poem, written by a German soldier in World War I, Hans Leip, and set to music by Rudolph Zink. It wasn't just popular in Germany, it was popular all over because it spoke to the yearnings of ordinary people for a return to happier times. Like everyone else, I loved that song. Many times I'd be making beds upstairs at the inn with the windows thrown wide. I'd be singing. People would hear me in the street below. They started calling me Lili Marleen.

೫

One of the reasons I was so happy to get a job where I lived out in the country was because food was more plentiful there.

The baker, who also happened to be *Frau* Esser's son-in-law, made frequent deliveries of fresh bread to the inn, arriving in his horse-drawn wagon.

People would come from *Köln* and the surrounding area and go house to house, or business to business, asking for food. They might get a potato here and a carrot there. By the time they were done, they'd have enough food for a meal.

I used to peel potatoes and shuck peas, sitting outside in front of the wash kitchen, which was housed in a barn-like structure, apart from the inn. This was also where the pigs were kept and the farm implements were stored. And it was where we heated water in a big pot once a week to take our baths.

Frau Esser one day said, "Wouldn't you like to go see your parents?" And of course, I loved going to

Gerda shucking peas at the inn in Kardorf

see my father. When I got back, the inn smelled so good! She had arranged for the butcher to come and slaughter the pig. During the war, this was against the law without a permit, so I guess they sent me away so I wouldn't know what they were doing.

The attic of the inn was huge. In one corner was a smokehouse, where they smoked the ham, made bacon and heavenly liver sausage and blood sausage. Today, I wouldn't touch blood sausage with a ten foot pole.

They made sour beans, too, in a huge crock covered with a cloth. The cloth was held in place

Chapter Three

with a rock, and over a period of several days the cloth would start to ferment, so I had to go down into the cellar every few days to change it out. Oh, that cellar scared me, because it was never finished, it was just like going down into the earth, you know. But the result was worth it. They were like French beans — they were heavenly.

There were some French prisoners of war housed in barracks not too far from the inn. Every day, the prisoners were assigned to work duty wherever they were needed. In the mornings we would hear them arrive. They wore wooden shoes, and we would hear their shoes click-clicking as they were being marched down the street toward the inn. One was assigned to *Frau* Esser, because she had fields that required tending. His name was George Dubedeaux. I sometimes worked beside him in the fields. Poor George! A prisoner slaving alongside a young German girl, who sometimes wore a bikini to work in on a hot summer day!

He received care packages from home and often brought me chocolates, but I never accepted them. You would never fraternize with the enemy! This was very frowned upon, and young ladies who did this were social outcasts, at best.

One day, he asked, "Do you have a cook pot I could use?" He used it to cook his snails! I never used that pot again!

Chapter Four

ONCE, A FRIEND of mine and I went by train to *Köln* to see *Cabaret*. Afterward, we stopped and visited my mother's parents, *Oma* (grandma) and *Opa* (grandpa) Lennartz.

I remember one of their bedrooms was off-limits. It was always kept ready for visits from my grandfather's brother, Mathieu, which happened every four years. He was a musician — played the cello with the Philadelphia Philharmonic Orchestra. Whenever he visited, it might as well have been the king who came, because they treated him like royalty. We were admonished, "Kids, be quiet! *Onkel* Mathieu is here from Philadelphia. So you just behave!"

Anyway, on this occasion we didn't stay very long. What we'd really stopped by for were matches. *Oma* was quick to give them to us. There had been a recent bombing raid in *Köln*, and dark is very dark when all the lights of the city are off to avoid being a

Chapter Four

Christina "Oma" Lennartz

target for Allied planes. *Oma* thought we wanted the matches to light our way. She offered us a candle. As soon as we left, we started giggling, because what we actually wanted them for was to light our cigarettes. We were just silly girls, back then, and didn't truly realize the seriousness of the situation.

I did, finally, see *Herr* Müller one more time. He had been drafted and was stationed in Euskirchen, about seventeen miles southwest of Bonn. He wrote to me, inviting me to visit him there. You wouldn't use the telephone at that time, unless it was absolutely necessary, because of the war. On every phone you would see a sign "*faße dich kurz*" (make it quick)! I was thrilled, of course! That night, I dressed up and he took me out to a very nice restaurant for dinner. Then we went to see the opera, *Tosca*.

If I had been enthralled with him before, I was even more so on that beautiful night. Perhaps he was simply putting a nice ending on an unfinished story, but for me the romance of it all took my childish infatuation to the next level, where it took on the deeper emotional characteristics of first love.

Alas, those feelings had nowhere to go. As the days and weeks went by without a word from him again, I buried those feelings and went on with my life. Later, I learned he bought a restaurant and bowling alley after the war and was busy running the business and taking care of his family.

Chapter Four

As time went on, more and more of the young men I dated wore uniforms. By 1943, I was seeing a young soldier from Austria. His name was Gustav. I called him Gustl. Gustl and I got along famously. He was in the *Panzer* (tank) division, under Rommel.

I remember our last evening together before he was shipped off to his next post. He said he wanted to marry me, and after he left he wrote to me faithfully. I was sure that I would one day be his wife, and that I'd end up living in Austria.

Little did I know how drastically my life was about to change.

Across the street from the inn lived a young woman. Marichen and I had become fast friends during my time in Kardorf. Her two children — one boy and one girl — were adorable!

It was such a sad time, though, because the Allies had begun in earnest making bombing runs to *Köln*, which was less than fifteen miles to the north.

The blare of sirens would alert us to the danger. I took her little girl and she took the boy. They were always fully dressed, because now it was happening nearly every night. We'd have to grab the children and run to a shelter dug into the hillside. It was cold, nasty and wet. It must have been terrifying for them. I know it was for me. When the sirens sounded again, that was the *entwarnung* (all-clear) that it was okay to come out. (As a bit of trivia, we used to wear our hair up in a hairdo we called *entwarnung*.)

Frau Esser also owned a large dance hall in Kardorf, right next to the inn. The townspeople used to come dancing, have parties. For a while the

German soldiers took it over as a barracks. They would come into the restaurant and bar at the inn. The officers were always very pushy and arrogant. They would come behind the bar and make advances. You would never say anything, of course. You just put up with it. No doubt, I would have been offended if they hadn't shown an interest.

One night, the dance hall was bombed. It was completely destroyed! Fortunatetly for them, the soldiers had been alerted the day before, so they were gone when it happened, but there were still many other casualties.

A make-shift hospital was set up in an underground bunker. *Frau* Esser's nieces, the baker's daughters, were among those badly injured. Their cries of pain and fear, mingled with those of the other wounded — many of them children — filled that small bunker and brought home to me the ugly reality of war in a way I hadn't experienced to that point.

After that, *Frau* Esser and I shared a room. Having this happen, literally so close to home, had left both of us very frightened. It was comforting to have each other's company as the reality of war encroached more and more each day.

As if things weren't bad enough, when *Frau* Esser's son came home on leave, he spotted me and asked his mother who I was.

She answered casually, "Oh, she's my maid."

Later, he cornered me in one of the upstairs guestrooms. Wearing a uniform can do strange things to some men. I think he was feeling self-important and

CHAPTER FOUR

powerful. There was no escaping him. He raped me. I felt disgusted and dirty and angry and frightened. I knew no one would believe me — certainly not *Frau* Esser! There was nothing I could do about it. Later, I found out he died on the Russian front.

After months of suffering the constant threat of air raids, *Frau* Esser could tell my nerves were wearing pretty thin. In the summer of 1944, she finally urged me to go east to join my sister. Many women with children had already gone to escape the bombings. My sister's husband was fighting somewhere in Russia. She was alone with their two children.

I went to my father in Bonn and asked him if he could help me get there. In his line of work, he had connections — people who were moving food supplies from here to there.

"But," he said, "I can only get you part way there. The last part of the journey, you will be on your own."

I actually ended up going much of the way by train. On the last leg, I was so exhausted — probably because I was so frightened — that I fell asleep.

When I woke up, the man across from me exclaimed, "You are so lucky you slept! When we went through Fulda, they were bombing it. It was terrible!"

Here I had come all this way to escape the bombing, but it seemed to have followed me!

It was nearly seven o'clock at night when the train pulled into the station at a little village in the Rhön Mountains. It was the closest stop to Hümpfershausen, where my sister was living. With several miles left to go, and no idea how I was going to get there, I went into a nearby café. Perhaps someone there would know how I could get to Hümpfershausen.

"You are in luck," a waitress told me. "Laborers from the *fabricken* (factory) are just getting off work. There is a bus that delivers them to their homes in the outlying villages. You can go with them."

The laborers were dirty and tired, but as we drove through the darkness, they started singing together to lift one another's spirits. My throat closed and the sum of all my exhaustion and fear was released in sympathetic tears.

Caught totally by surprise — there'd been no way to communicate with her before I came — my sister was stunned to see me when I knocked on her door. Then she wrapped her arms around me and hugged me so tight! "How on earth did you get here?"

I'll never forget that first night in Hümpfershausen: Christel and her two boys, Hans and Jup (nickname for Josef) lived in a single room with a pot-bellied stove. The boys slept in their crib and Christel made room for me in the single bed. A short time after we'd settled down to sleep, I heard a humming overhead.

"Christel," I whispered, "What is that noise?"

"Those are enemy planes on their way to bomb Berlin."

"What! I thought we were supposed to be safe here from the bombing!"

"Don't worry, they won't bomb us," she assured me. "They don't bother the tiny villages."

Nevertheless, no one in Hümpfershausen ever tempted fate by leaving their lights on at night, unless the windows were well-draped with heavy curtains.

CHAPTER FOUR

Hümpfershausen is a small, rural village. On the outskirts of town is a place called Schloss Sinnershausen. From the thirteenth to early sixteenth centuries there was a monastery on that site. It was destroyed during the Peasant's War in 1525, when peasant farmers in the area rebelled against increasing demands placed upon them by the aristocrats who benefited from their labors. Locally, those taskmasters were the monks. The peasants demolished the monastery and the monks abandoned it. After the rebellion was put down, the people of the town were sentenced to death and the town itself — Lücker Hausen — was burned. It no longer exists. Hümpfershausen grew up nearby.

In the 1600's, three women were tried as witches in Hümpfershausen. One was burned at the stake.

For a short time, I stayed with Christel. Every morning, we had to get up and cautiously work our way around some ill-tempered geese to get to the woodpile. We'd chop the wood and carry it in to stoke up the fire. That pot-bellied stove smoked liked crazy!

Christel did all she could to acquire extra rations. In addition to that, my clothes were worn and my shoes were worse, so she went to the *Bürgermeister* (mayor) and lobbied for a certificate to buy me a pair of shoes, which I desperately needed. He was won over by her pretty smile and shapely figure. I got my shoes.

It was obvious there was not enough room for me to stay there very long. I was going to have to find a job and a place to live. There were no jobs to be had in the village, but down in Meiningen I found a position cleaning house for a man and wife who were both important doctors. They had a large, beautiful home and they had plenty of food to put on the table. Often their patients paid them with meat or produce from their farms.

In addition to my pay, they gave me room and board. It was a lovely room in their main house, but the best part was that I was welcomed at their table. *Frau* Doctor was a fabulous cook! I couldn't have fallen into a better situation. One day, she cooked a meal from venison, called rehrücken. It is a deer's back. She inserted slices of bacon in cuts along the back and, when it was done, presented it with a rich sauce. It was out of this world delicious!

They had two little children. One of my responsibilities was to make them breakfast every morning: *haferflocken* (oatmeal) with raisins. I rather liked it, myself, and to this day, I still have a bowl of oatmeal — with bananas — for breakfast each day.

I wrote to Gustl so he would know how to reach me. Every day, I went to the post office to see if I'd received a letter from him. Finally, I was much relieved when a letter arrived, and for the next several months our correspondence continued as it had before.

One night, *Frau* Doctor said, "Miss Gerda, are you smoking?"

I was, but I said, "*Nein, nein, nein!*" because she wouldn't allow that, but I was young and pleasures were few and far between at the time.

On an afternoon in March of 1945, *Frau* Doctor came to me. "I don't want you to worry, Gerda, but Hitler has ordered that all the bridges be blown up."

CHAPTER FOUR

This was, of course, intended to slow the enemy's advance. By this time, the Allies had broken through Hitler's Westwall, the series of bunkers, pillboxes and fortified positions which were built along Germany's western border before the war began. The Allies called it the Sigfried Line.

Though it was known to very few Germans, at the time — Hitler kept a tight lid on unfavorable news — Allied troops had, in fact, taken Bonn.

"You will probably hear some explosions," *Frau* Doctor continued, "but it is nothing for you to worry about."

But I did worry.

More than just the bridges were destroyed. Hitler knew it was all over. He wanted nothing left of value for the invading Allies. Industry, agriculture, communication, food supplies — he ordered everything destroyed.

A week or so later, with the Americans fast approaching from the west and the Russians moving in from the east, I took off on foot, making my way to Hümpfershausen.

The distance was probably about eight miles. My shoes crunched on the frosty ground. As I walked along the country road through the rural countryside, I heard an enemy plane overhead. It was common for them to dive down when they saw people in the fields. This had happened to me once before, at *Frau* Esser's, when George and I were digging potatoes. Sure enough, the pilot dove down, and it scared me so much, I fell into the ditch at the side of the road

A short while later, I nearly stumbled into an American encampment! As I crept away, I realized there was a man following me. He was the first black man I had ever seen. He was probably just making sure I didn't pose a threat, but I had no idea what his motives might be. I was terrified!

When I reached my sister, I pleaded with her to agree that it was time to go back to Bonn. We'd heard such awful stories about how German women were treated by the Russians. It was far preferable to go west and take our chances with the Americans.

It had been some time since Christel had heard from her husband, Heinz. When the southeastern front collapsed, many soldiers were taken prisoner and forced into slave labor in Russia. Christel was reluctant to leave without knowing what had happened to him. Was he dead or alive?

The Americans took over Meiningen. And what an unexpected treasure they discovered! It was there that the central records were kept for all United Nations prisoners of war held in Germany. Those records revealed the fate of hundreds of thousands of Allied personnel captured during the course of the war.

They commandeered *Frau* Doctor's house, relegating her and her husband to the garden shed. I knew they would be angry with me that I had gone off without saying a word. I didn't want to face *Frau* Doctor, but I'd left all my things there, so I convinced Christel to go down to pick them up.

When she returned with my belongings, she told me the Americans had trashed the house and that

CHAPTER FOUR

Frau Doctor was at her wits end. But my mind was made up. I wasn't going back there. In fact, I had been paid about thirty marks a month for my work, and every time I got paid I would go to the Meiningen bank, but I never saw any of that money again. I never took it out, because we just wanted to get out of there — to go home again.

In the couple of weeks that followed, while we were still in Hümpfershausen, we made the best of the crowded accommodations, but things were looking pretty bleak.

Under the circumstances, it's not surprising I heard no more from Gustl.

One day, someone came running through the streets shouting that a *fallschirm* (parachute) of supplies had fallen in Hümpfershausen. It must have gone slightly astray. Everyone turned out to tear into the package and take what they could get their hands on, but then an American military vehicle showed up and a man with a bullhorn warned us all that we would be arrested if we didn't return everything at once. It was so hard to relinquish our treasures, but no one wanted to test their resolve, so the townspeople brought everything back.

On another occasion, we heard that an American plane had crashed in a nearby field. We all went to gape at it and at the men who were just sitting there in shock. We didn't offer to help. All we wanted was to see what they looked like, as if maybe they had two heads or four arms. But there was nothing remarkably different about them. I have no idea what happened to those men or to the remains of their plane.

In the evenings, Christel and I would sing. We were great singers. She sang first voice, and I was always second voice. Our singing touched the heart of the lady who rented us the room; she cried, because her sons had been killed in the war.

Finally, though she still hadn't heard anything from or about Heinz, my sister agreed that it was time to head home. We had no money, but we were determined to get there, so we loaded the children into their buggy, stuffed it with as many of our things as it could carry, hung our copper cook pots on either side...and walked!

There were hundreds of people on the roads heading west. It was one of the largest migrations in history. People were terrified of the Russians and desperate to get as far away from their incursion as possible. Russian soldiers had been given free license by their superiors to do with the Germans as they pleased — and the harsher the better — in retribution for the damage done by the German military on their soil. No woman was too young or too old to be savaged by Russian soldiers.

On this journey, sometimes we were lucky enough to hitch a ride with a farmer on his wagon. One time, I was up front with the farmer; Christel and the children were riding in the wagon. Apparently, she accidentally sat on the wooden brake handle and broke it, thereby falling off the wagon into the middle of the road. She started shouting to get our attention. The farmer was pretty angry that she had broken his brake handle! He left us right there in the middle of

Chapter Four

the road and went on his way, muttering and shaking his head.

Once in a while, we would take a chance on getting help from people who lived in farmhouses along the way. They would give us a bit of food and perhaps let us spend the night in their barn. But many times we just had to make camp out in the open. We would put our meager scraps of food together in the cooking pot, cover it with some water and cook it over a fire to make what passed for a soup.

On Sunday, though, Christel said, "You know what? It's Sunday. Today, I'm going to ask for cake!"

I couldn't believe what I was hearing! "Cake? We are lucky to get anything!" But that was Christel.

Christel favored Hans, her oldest son, and I liked little Jup. One time, we got into a fight about a kettle of soup. She had ladled out more for Hans than she had for his brother.

I said, "You've given Hans more than you've given to little Jup!"

She took the kettle and tossed it into the air — threw the whole thing away! None of us had anything to eat that night.

American tanks passed us on the road from time to time. They never bothered us. The soldiers smiled and waved and shouted, "Hi, Blondie! Want chocolate?" They didn't seem frightening at all!

It took us ten days to get back to Bonn. What we found there was shocking. Of course, the beautiful bridge had been destroyed. The towers in the middle were piles of rubble and the main span was a mangled mess, partially submerged in the river.

Above and below: 1945 Bonn Rheinbrücke

1945 A street near the bridge in Bonn

Chapter Four

To move men and supplies across the *Rhein*, the Allies had built what was called a pontoon bridge — a flat, temporary structure supported by boat-like floats. Later, they would build the bridge that spans the river today between Bonn and Beuel — a much more modern version — once again affixing the irreverent statue of the boy on the east end, pointing his bottom at Beuel. It was renamed Kennedybrücke ten days after President Kennedy's assassination, in 1963.

Christel and I weren't allowed to cross the pontoon bridge to Bonn until we had been sprayed with delousing chemicals. All the refugees were subjected to this. Since we'd all spent several days in the same clothes, sleeping on the ground or in barns, I guess it was understandable, but it was, nonetheless, demeaning.

Our father and stepmother were living in a single room — their apartment building had been destroyed! We also learned that our father's sister, *Tante* Anna — not to be confused with his sister-in-law *Tante* Änne — had been killed in the bombing of *Köln* on June 29, 1943. Her only son, Ferdie, was killed a couple of weeks later, in Russia, but she wasn't there to receive the telegram informing her of his death.

My father was called in to identify her body. His duty, at the time, was to scour the rubble for survivors — more often he found the remains of those who had been killed — a truly gruesome task. My mother's father, my *Opa* Lennartz, too, was killed in the bombing of *Köln*, but they never found his body. *Oma* Lennartz survived. She later went to live with my mother's twin brother, Rudolf.

One of the treasures I brought with me from Bonn to America was an item my father found in the rubble of Kassel, another bombed-out city he was sent to, in northern Germany. He said it came from what was once a beautiful, upscale neighborhood — it is the statue I have of two monkeys. They are huddled together, looking very sad and frightened. On the bottom is written — by whom I have no idea — "Moritz", and I have to wonder if the statue was inspired by the German illustrated tales of Max and Moritz, by Wilhelm Busch in the early 1830's.

Chapter Five

Germany surrendered on May 8, 1945. The war was officially over! Even as Christel and I tried to get resituated, Germany was being divided into occupation zones.

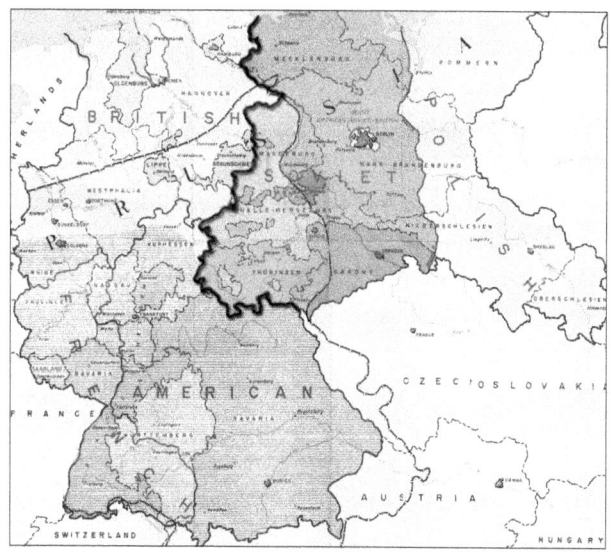

Hümpfershausen, and the whole state of Thuringen, was in the Russian-occupied zone. It would later fall within the boundaries of "East Germany". Thank goodness we didn't stay there!

Bonn was in the English zone, but there were American soldiers there, too, for a while.

Christel went to live with her in-laws in Beuel, still anxiously waiting to learn the fate of her husband, and for a while I had no other choice but to stay with my father and stepmother.

Germany had lost the war, but the German people were much relieved by the end of hostilities. Before it was over, many Germans had even come to the point where they were wishing someone would kill Hitler, just so the war would come to an end.

Now, there was an air of renewed hope and, for young girls, the flood of Allied forces brought new and interesting men into the picture. The war had decimated the young male population of Germany. Many were being held in POW camps, either by the Western Allies or, far worse and far longer, in enforced labor camps in Russia. Those who were lucky enough to return to their homes were completely demoralized.

No word arrived from Gustl. I had no idea what had happened to him. Of course, I thought the worst.

At twenty-one years old, I was not immune to the attraction of American soldiers. I dated one by the name of Raymond a couple of times, but then he just seemed to disappear.

On Viktoriastraße one day, I was standing there talking with my friend, Millie, when we saw a young American soldier with stripes on his shoulders.

Chapter Five

The stripes reminded me of the ones on Raymond's uniform, so I nudged Millie and told her we should ask this soldier about Raymond. She said she knew the guy, and she would introduce me to him.

That is how I met Paul.

I asked this tall, handsome American soldier if he knew where Raymond was. He told me Raymond had been shipped home.

Then he said, "Blondie, would you like to meet me sometime?"

I was flattered, and of course I said, "Yes!"

German girls were entranced by American soldiers. There was such an aura of celebrity about them. They were brash and confident. I don't suppose any of us gave a thought to the fact that we were playing with fire. One girl I knew got mixed up with a couple of different soldiers and got pregnant both times. Neither offered marriage. She wasn't able to take care of the children, so they ended up in an orphanage.

Paul and I got to know each other by taking long walks in the parks. We both enjoyed hiking, and Paul could speak enough German for us to communicate very well. He was so intelligent! That was one of the things I liked best about him. Talk about fairy tales! I felt like I'd met my Prince Charming!

He was born April 23, 1918, in Portland, Oregon. His father was a locomotive engineer for Southern Pacific Railroad. After Paul graduated from Benson Polytechnic, he did four years of apprenticeship with the railroad and then got his master machinist card.

CHAPTER FIVE

When the U.S. got involved in the war, Paul was working full-time for the railroad. He volunteered for service and by 1943 found himself assigned with the rank of sergeant to Company "B" of the 740th Operating Battalion. Arriving in Mayenne on the heels of the retreating German troops, they found the rail lines a tangled mess of steel, with battered engines and rail cars lying on their sides.

Their responsibility was to re-establish rail transportation as quickly as possible, in concert with the Allied push through France, Belgium and Holland, and to keep all the rolling stock in operation up to the battle lines.

They experienced some of the most harrowing conditions in Liege, Belgium, where they worked under the constant threat of buzz bombings and strafing. It was there that Paul took a piece of shrapnel in his scalp, and that's how close we came to not having this story to write.

No Enemy of Mine

The determined efforts of the 740th Operating Battalion were essential to supplying the ammunition, rations and gasoline which allowed forces under General George Patton's command to take Paris and continue the advancement through the Siegfried Line into Germany.

When Hitler started building the Sigfried Line in 1938, it caused a lot of unease in Europe, and at the start of the war, Ulster song-writer, Jimmy Kennedy, wrote what became a very popular song among the Allied troops: "We're Going to Hang Out the Washing on the Sigfried Line".

Breaking through that line was the result of a hard-won victory over German troops in the Battle of the Bulge.

1945 Paul "hanging on the Sigfried Line"

So, when Paul had his picture taken somewhere along that line, in front of a field of what were called

CHAPTER FIVE

"dragon's teeth", he wrote on the back of it: "Me hanging on the Sigfried Line". "Dragon's teeth" were concrete fortifications, usually laced with landmines.

At the time we met, Paul was living out of a boxcar, the soldiers' temporary quarters as they were being moved from place to place.

Paul outside the boxcar barracks

Boxcar barracks interior

When I saw the tattoos on his arm, I thought, He must be a tough guy, because only tough guys have tattoos! Paul had three: an American eagle, the American flag and his Social Security number.

Before long, I was seeing him exclusively. Paul loved to go places and see things. On one occasion, he asked me if I would like to go to *Köln*, on a sort of pilgrimage to see the ruins left by the bombing that had taken the lives of my grandfather and aunt.

Köln was still smoldering. During the course of the war, the city was bombed 262 times, killing approximately twenty thousand people! The last one was in March, 1945. More than eight hundred planes dropped their bombs. The devastation was massive; piles and piles of rubble everywhere!

1945 Devastation in Köln (Cologne), Germany

I imagined what it must have been like for *Tante* Anna in those last moments. And was my *Opa* still lying somewhere under all that debris? I remembered

Chapter Five

the kind old man taking my sister and me to the movies — and I cried.

It wasn't long after that when something happened to cast a brief shadow over our relationship. A young boy, who hung around the boxcars hoping for candy or other handouts, approached me one day with a snide little smile on his face.

"He's married," the boy said cryptically.

I said, "What?"

"Yeah, he's married! He has a wife back in America."

Totally stunned, I turned and ran. Paul ran after me and finally managed to calm me down. I had no idea why the boy would tell me such a nasty lie, but I believed Paul when he insisted what the boy had said was not true.

We always had such a lovely time together, and one night we pushed the boundaries of curfew just beyond its limits. Paul had just kissed me good-night underneath the lamplight at the big gate in front of my parents' apartment building. For a moment, I felt like Lili Marleen. I could almost hear Lale Anderson's sultry voice singing the words "underneath the lantern by the barracks gate…"

The mood was rudely shattered, though. As Paul began to walk away, a British MP strode up and took me by the arm.

"You're under arrest," he said, "for violating curfew."

It was just a minute or two past ten o'clock, but the British soldiers felt some animosity toward the

"Yanks" when it came to women, so he was being spiteful.

I learned later that Paul burst into my father and step-mother's bedroom and shone a flashlight in Dad's eyes. He was ranting that he would get me back; that he would deliver me safely home. Dad was pretty angry — not so much because I had been thrown in jail, but because Paul had barged into his bedroom and shone a light in his eyes!

Even though it was late at night, Paul went to the American Consul and arranged for my release. He was very determined, you know, and he felt very bad that he had gotten me into this predicament.

After spending several hours in a cell with three other women, finally, someone said, "Is your name Gerda?"

"Yes," I said through my tears.

Paul was raising quite a stir running up and down the blocks of cells, waving those release papers and calling my name. I was so impressed that he would go to such lengths to get me out of there. In later years, he would say jokingly, "That was the biggest mistake I ever made!"

ෆ

I needed to find a job again, now that I was back in Bonn. My parents' apartment was too small to include me for very long, and I wasn't keen on staying there with them, anyway. Although I eagerly renewed my friendship with Marichen, my friend from Kardorf,

Chapter Five

I had no desire to resume the job with *Frau* Esser; I now had a good reason to stay in Bonn.

Instead, I found a job at a bakery, and they gave me a tiny room on the third floor, overlooking the city. I loved it there, especially when the church bells rang, filling the air with a cacophony of sound! I had heard them so many times before, but now I heard them with so much more appreciation. It was good to be home!

When Paul presented me with the ring I still wear to this day, I had no idea of its significance. It was a diamond, but in Germany it is traditional to give a girl a gold band for engagement, which she wears on her left hand until she is married — then the band moves over to the right hand. It wasn't as if he had actually proposed, so I was totally unaware. I thought it was just a pretty ring that he was giving me as a gift.

One day, I discovered the diamond was missing from my ring. I often took it off while I was cleaning and left it hanging on a hook in my room.

I was frantic! In desperation I approached my stepbrother, Willy, for help.

Willy had gotten pretty high in the German army before the war was over. Afterwards, he had a tough time finding a job. No one wanted to hire him, because of his rank during the war. So my father got him started in the produce market. With his intelligence, he immediately did very well. He married a woman who was a few years older than himself.

He knew how to get things on the black market. There was no other way.

He said, "You meet me tonight. Here is the place. Bring cigarettes, as many cartons as you can."

At that time you could buy nothing with money. Money wasn't worth anything, but cigarettes and things that you could trade, those were worth something. I told Paul what had happened and he came up with enough cigarettes to make the deal.

☙

The day finally came when he was being shipped back to the States. He was very unhappy about having to leave me, but at that time it wasn't permitted for a German girl to marry an American soldier.

As we were saying goodbye, he reached into his pocket and pulled out an envelope, which he handed to me. With one last kiss, he was gone. Inside the envelope was a letter and four hundred dollars, which was a considerable sum at that time in Germany. The letter read:

> *Whatever you may do, wherever you may go, remember that I love you with all my heart and I am coming back for you as soon as I can.*
> *All my love, Paul*

I didn't really believe him. Out of sight, out of mind, I thought. Lots of soldiers pledged their love and never returned, so my skepticism was not without justification.

Weeks and months passed.

Chapter Five

In the meantime, I found a higher-paying job, cleaning house for a well-known doctor and his family. They were related to a family that owned a big department store chain in Germany, like Macy's here. It seemed I was always fortunate to find good positions with well-to-do people. The doctor and his family treated me very well, and I was always invited to eat at their table with them, as if I, too, were a member of the family.

The lady I worked for noticed the ring on my finger, one day, and exclaimed, "Gertrud, you are *verlobt* (engaged)!"

I said, "What?"

She said, "Yes, Gertrud, you are wearing an engagement ring!" I had no idea! But she was a woman of the world. She knew about the American tradition of giving a diamond ring.

The German men I ran into didn't know what it was, either. They would still ask me out, so I asked my stepbrother, Willy — the one who spoke seven languages fluently — to teach me how to say, "Around the corner is my house. My fiancé waits for me."

Christel, too, was still waiting for her husband. There had been no word. Just about the time she began to accept that Heinz must have been killed — a little less than a year after the war was over — Heinz finally returned home. He had been in a Russian prison. Nobody recognized him; he was like a skeleton! They had starved and beaten him! It was such a miracle to have him back with us! Hans and Jup would have a chance to get to know their father.

One afternoon, *Frau* Doctor sent me with her youngest daughter, Elisabeth, into the country by train to get potatoes. We had to walk a mile to the farmhouse to pick them up. Being young and curious, when we got to the farm we looked around and spotted a chicken's nest full of eggs.

"Oh, my, Elisabeth, look at the eggs!" I said, "Shall we take one?"

She said, "Oh, yes!"

So, we each took one. But within moments I felt so guilty about stealing, I couldn't stand it!

"Elisabeth, let's take them back!" We went back and returned them to the nest.

The potatoes came in a big bag; they weighed about fifty pounds! We had to carry that bag from the farm to the train station, about a mile away, hefting it between us a few yards at a time; each time setting it down to catch our breaths.

After a while, I grew tired of doing nothing but work; of having no fun at all. For all I knew, Paul was never coming back. So, when my cousin, Gertrude asked me if I would go dancing at the English soldiers' club, I bargained with her to let me wear her pink Angora sweater. I paid heavily for that. She had beautiful clothes, and I had very few clothes at all.

It was a great time! I learned to jitterbug!

Chapter Six

THE DAY PAUL finally returned, I heard the doorbell ring and a man's voice speaking with the doctor's daughter. I remember the sound of her footsteps as she crossed the hall and entered the room where I was working.

"Gertrud, there is an American soldier asking for you!"

I knew at once that it was Paul!

I flew to the door and straight into his arms! Oh, it was so good to see him! I couldn't believe he had come back for me! In fact, he'd had to re-enlist to accomplish it!

His unit had just arrived in Germany and was being moved by train south to the American occupation zone. He had begged his commanding officer to let him get off the train in Bonn to see me. His CO gave him permission, with the understanding that he must be back on the train the next day, before it left Bonn for Wiesbaden, or he would be considered AWOL (absent without leave).

He told me how much he'd missed me, and shortly after his return, he even wrote a piece protesting the prohibition of marriage between GI's and their sweethearts. It was published in the military newspaper, *Stars and Stripes*.

> '. . . I, Too, Fell in Love'
>
> Yes, I was here during combat days and saw my buddies killed by German bullets and bombs. At the same time we were told that we were fighting for the "Four Freedoms"—"Freedom of Speech," "Freedom of Religion," "Freedom from Fear" and "Freedom from Want."
>
> "Freedom of Speech" I am exercising now; "Freedom of Religion" every Sunday; but "Freedom from Fear" and "Freedom from Want"—I don't know.
>
> You see, I, too, fell in love with a German girl and, after going back to the States and being discharged, I found that I couldn't forget her, so here I am back again, hoping and praying that someday soon the Army will recognize that when a man and woman fall in love they should be permitted to marry regardless of nationalities.
>
> When that happy day comes then other GIs and myself will know "Freedom from Fear"—the fear that you'll never be able to provide for your loved one in a way befitting Democracy; and the "Freedom from Want"—the want that eats into your heart and soul when you want a woman for your wife and can't have her, because a GI isn't to have a heart when it comes to falling in love with a good, clean German girl. —Sgt. P. A. M.

When Paul became aware that young German men were oblivious to what the diamond ring on my hand meant, he had his mother send over a gold band. It is the wedding band I still wear, although now, sixty-eight years later, it is worn very thin.

Paul's new assignment was at Camp Taylor, in Freudenberg, on the hill above Wiesbaden. He was in charge of the motor pool. He came to see me every weekend, travelling by train from Wiesbaden to Beuel, then taking the ferry across the *Rhein* to Bonn. Until the bridge could be rebuilt, all travelers had to cross by boat.

CHAPTER SIX

Camp Taylor at Feudenberg

Ferry between Bonn and Beuel

On the return trip, he would give the engineer on the train a package of cigarettes, if he would slow down a little at Schierstein so Paul could jump off. If he had to go all the way to Wiesbaden, he would have to backtrack a couple of miles before hiking up the hill to Freudenberg.

One time, he wasn't able to get enough time off to come see me, so I decided I was going to go to him. This wasn't as easy as it might sound. In order to cross zones, you had to have a permit. This was something I did not have, but I didn't let that stop me.

I boarded the train in Bonn and managed to elude the authorities, who were checking for passes, by getting off the train at every stop and slipping back into one of the cars before it continued on. There were lots of American soldiers on the train. They were drunk and rowdy and they gave me a pretty hard time — a young, single German woman alone in their midst. At first, when we reached Wiesbaden, they weren't going to let me get off, but I pleaded with them and they finally did.

Train station at Wiesbaden

Chapter Six

There was a young man at the train stop. He was pushing two bicycles. I asked him where he was going. He said he was going as far as Schierstein, part of the way to Freudenberg. It worked out for both of us, because he let me ride one of the bicycles, which saved me from having to walk all the way, and by letting me ride it he didn't have to manage both bicycles at the same time.

From Schierstein I had to walk up the hill a couple of miles to the *kaserne* (barracks) at Freudenberg. Freudenberg means "Happy Hill". Several Army jeeps passed me along the way, many of them driven by women from the Women's Army Corp. They looked so capable and confident. I wanted to be like them.

Someday, I'll drive a car, I thought to myself.

By the time I reached Freudenberg, it was starting to get dark, and I realized I had nowhere to stay! I had nothing! My only focus had been just getting to where Paul was stationed. But, I was in luck: here came an elderly couple out for their evening walk.

I said, "Do you know where I can stay for the night? I'm here to see my fiancé."

And they said, "Oh, yes, girl, you can stay with us!"

The next morning, I approached the *kaserne* and asked one of the soldiers in front, "Could you get Paul McMillan, my fiancé?" And so he did.

It was a beautiful get together. I stayed a few days with that lovely couple who had given me shelter.

Then I was presented with the problem of how to get back home. I was on the American side and I had to get back to the English side, or else go through the whole process of getting on and off the train to avoid detection when they checked for a pass that I didn't possess. Somebody said there was a man with a little boat who would take you across the river, if you paid him with cigarettes or chocolate. And that's what I did.

While we were in the middle of the *Rhein* River, here comes this big American excursion boat. It generated large waves that tossed our little boat around crazily. I was so scared! That was a horrible trip, but we finally made it to the other side. I waded through the mud to the shore and then had to catch a train in the English zone, back to Bonn.

After a few weeks of making the trip back and forth between Freudenberg and Bonn, Paul asked me to move to Wiesbaden, to be closer to him.

When I told my boss in Bonn that I was no longer going to work there, and that when Paul and I got married we would be moving to the American west, she looked horrified and exclaimed, "Oh my, they still have Indians there!"

I actually found a place to live in Dotzheim, further up toward Freudenberg. It was very convenient. My landlady was an older woman by the name of *Frau* Rôth.

Wiesbaden is a spa city, built on thermal springs. It is quite beautiful. Paul used to take me to the *Kurhaus* (cure house), which was a fabulous spa. Since he planned to take me with him to America, I was given a pass that allowed me to go into the fancy spa restaurant every Sunday for lunch.

Chapter Six

View of Wiesbaden from Camp Taylor

Kurhaus in Wiesbaden

We stayed in Dotzheim for about a year-and-a-half. My little apartment was very simple, but I made it my own. I was very comfortable there, even though there weren't many amenities.

Dotzheim

The neighbors were such wonderful people. My friend, Tilchen, lived downstairs in the building next door, and in the apartment above her a woman named Bubble lived with her husband and son.

None of us had a bathroom, but the neighbors took in laundry, so they had a laundry room. On Saturdays, in cooler weather, all of us women — Tilchen, Bubble and myself — would go into the laundry room, heat some water and take our baths. Bubble had a little boy, Peter, who was about five years old. Here we were all naked in little tubs and young Peter was peeping in through the window to watch us.

In the summertime, though, we made bathing an event! We wore bathing suits and filled a big tub out in the yard.

Chapter Six

Outside the motor pool at Camp Taylor

Bath time

Paul and Peter were always kind of playing around. There was a little balcony we had to walk under to go into the apartment, so one day Peter ran up onto the balcony and, as Paul came through, he poured a bucket of water over him! Thankfully, Paul had a good sense of humor.

Every weekend, the women baked either a huge prune cake or an apple cake. Oh, the smell was fabulous! Because their own ovens were not large enough for the big pans, the women would just walk down to the bakery to have them baked. It was an old tradition. We cooked with coal — they called them briquettes.

That's one thing I'm sorry I missed out on, not having a mother who cooked or baked. My mother worked long hours in the market, so there wasn't time for baking or sewing or any of the other domestic skills other girls learned from their mothers. My cousin's mother could cook, bake or can anything, and she passed this knowledge to her daughter. I envied my cousin because of her mother baking and doing all those things; she envied me because I always got to go to the delicatessen!

Once in a while, Tilchen and I would take the little train that ran from Wiesbaden up Neroberg hill. Sometimes it was snowing, and I'd wonder how the little train could get up the track without sliding back down. But we would go there because it was the only place around that had beef. We loved beef tenderloin and there was a butcher's shop up there in the village where our neighbor's daughter lived. Later, I learned how the train worked. It is really interesting! This

CHAPTER SIX

train started operating in 1888. Two cars are attached to one another by cables. Tanks in the car at the top of the tracks are filled with water so that when it begins its downward journey the weight of it pulls the car at the bottom of the hill up the tracks. So simple, but so ingenious!

Paul loved to explore and we both loved to hike, so we took many little side trips while we lived in Wiesbaden. One of these was an excursion by boat down the *Rhein*. Most rivers flow south, but the *Rhein* flows north.

Castle along the Rhein

Koblenz

Koblenz

Koblenz pontoon bridge across river

Chapter Six

We saw so many castles, bombed out cities and the remains of several bridges that were destroyed during the war.

Another castle along the Rhein

Ludendorf Bridge

Sometimes we would take the train all the way to Waldorf and walk back as far as Kardorf to see Marichen. We would return home carrying bags heavy with fresh meat and produce from the country.

Packing back our treasures from Waldorf

One of our trips was to Frankfort. Paul took me there in an open Jeep. It was a cold, blustery day. My hair flapped around my face like the wings of a fettered bird desperate to escape.

I caught a terrible cold that ultimately landed me in the hospital. From my bed, looking out the window, I could see a beautiful building across the street. I learned that it had been a *lebensborn* facility. Literally translated, *lebensborn* means "birth", or "spring of life". This was the first I'd heard of the program, established by the SS during the war and supported

CHAPTER SIX

by Hitler. Extra-marital relations were encouraged between "racially pure and healthy" German men and women for the purpose of raising the birthrate of Aryan children, who would then presumably grow up to serve the *Reich*.

Patient care in the hospital was performed by nuns. I remember calling over the one assigned to me, beseeching her for more medicine and wailing that I was going to die! I suppose I was frightened because my mother had died of pneumonia.

But the pragmatic German nun just scoffed and said, "Ach! You don't die that easily! You're already green from the medicine I've given you!"

☙

Under the War Brides Act, which finally went into effect on December 28, 1945 — shortly after Paul returned from the States — the non-Asian spouses, natural children, and adopted children of United States military personnel were now allowed to enter the U.S. Actually making it happen wasn't all that easy. It involved completing pages and pages of application forms, a series of lab tests and medical examinations, and then weeks and weeks of waiting.

The end of Paul's second tour was rapidly approaching. One month before he was due to leave, we finally got permission to marry. Being Catholic, I, of course, wanted to be married in the church, but Paul convinced me we should have a simple wedding in Germany and then do it up right when we got to America.

Of course, I didn't haven't anything much, so Paul's mother sent me some beautiful clothes from the States. The shoes were much too big, but I didn't care. With a little newspaper stuffed inside, they were just fine. And so we were married at the *Standesamt* (City Hall) by an Army Justice of the Peace on May 27, 1948. I had no flowers, but the wonderful neighbors we had — my friends — brought me the most gorgeous bouquet of my favorite flower: peonies.

Mr. and Mrs. McMillan

We had a party with our friends in Wiesbaden and then another party in Bonn, with my family and friends there. At one point during the evening, I noticed my father was missing. I went to find him. He'd been drinking — that hadn't changed — and he was feeling very emotional. His little girl was going far away, and he had no idea whether he would ever see her again. He'd left the room because he didn't want anyone to see that he was crying.

Däddy, Gerda, Paul, Dad, stepmother, Willy

Clockwise from bottom left: Jup and Gertrud, Marichen and Tony, Gerda and Paul, Christel and Josef

For the next few weeks, we just kept going back and forth to Bonn to see my parents. Paul had bought a used Volkswagen from another soldier who had already gone back to the States, and on one of these trips to Bonn the axle broke. We were way out in the country; nothing around but a farm house. They had wood stacked up in front of their place, so Paul asked if he could have some of it. He was always very handy, so he jerry-rigged them under the car and we were able to go a few miles before all the wood fell out; he put it back in and we continued in this fashion until we got into the next town to a service station.

During these last visits, I enjoyed once again walking beside my Dad along the *Rhein* as he wheeled his bicycle. We were very companionable with one another; both of us realizing moments like these were unlikely to come again.

Gerda and Paul and their Volkswagen

Chapter Six

Chapter Seven

Finally, the day arrived when the great American adventure began!

Unforgettable! Traveling from Wiesbaden to Bremerhaven was an overnight trip. We had bunk beds, and I kept jumping to the window every five minutes saying, "Where are we now? Where are we now?" you know, like an impatient child.

But I was so lucky, and I knew it. I truly felt like I was living in a fairy tale! So many girls — some with children — were never going to get to go to America. Their soldiers had left them behind.

We stayed three days in Bremerhaven and, ah, it was like heaven, because of all the wonderful food they had to offer in the soldiers' mess hall! They had chocolate and canned bacon and spam! I loved fried spam! Today, these things would not sound like luxuries, but then they sure were to me!

Only one thing marred our time together there: Paul wanted to take a walk along the waterfront one

CHAPTER SEVEN

afternoon. I wasn't feeling well, so I declined. But that didn't stop him. In fact, he went accompanied by an attractive woman from the Women's Army Corp! I was so upset I worked myself up until I was really sick.

The next day, I said to Paul, "Take me to the harbor. Let me see the ship." I was so afraid of going across the ocean. There were two ships there in the harbor.

"Which ship is it?" I asked. And of course I was hoping it would be the big one and not the small one. Well, it was the small one.

The ships were all named after generals; ours was the *USAT General Edwin D. Patrick*. She didn't start out with that name, though. She was originally built as an Admiral class Navy transport vessel, with the long-term purpose of becoming a passenger liner. The ship was originally commissioned the *USS Admiral C. F. Hughes*. When the war ended she was decommissioned and transferred to the Army Transportation Service. The *General Edwin D. Patrick* was just under 609 feet long, a little more than 75 feet wide and had a draft of 26.6 feet. Her maximum speed was 19 knots.

USAT General Edwin M. Patrick

Soldiers were housed on the lower level, the WACs (Women's Army Corp) were on the second level and spouses and children were on the upper level. Women with no children were put together, three or four of us in each stateroom. At first, I thought the women I bunked with were American — they spoke English very well! But they were German girls, smart enough to realize it would benefit them to learn English before they went to America. I was not so smart. Because Paul spoke excellent German, I'd never felt the need to learn much English.

I honestly think I filled the North Sea with my tears when we left the harbor, because all I could see was my father standing there. He wasn't there, really, but in my mind I could see him there, waving goodbye. And they played this song — I didn't know what the words meant at the time, "Should auld acquaintance be forgot...", but the mournful sound of it, ah, that brought the tears. This is it, you know?

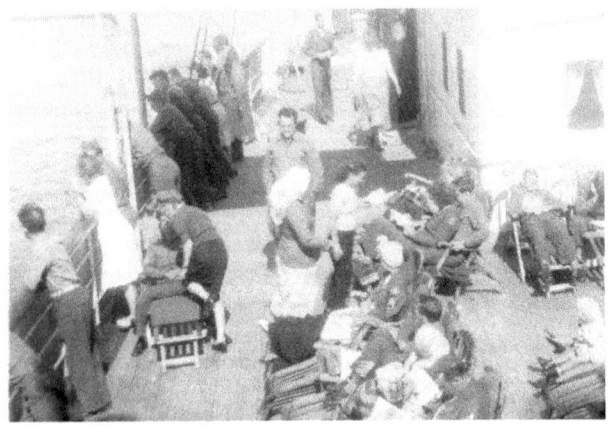

1948 Passengers aboard the MM Patrick

Chapter Seven

The North Sea was very rough. I got sick…laid low, I thought, by the motion of the ship as it rose and fell on the big swells.

The ship made two stops before crossing the Atlantic: one in Scotland and the next in Southampton, England. Of course we did not get a chance to do any sight-seeing. We stayed aboard ship as they took on supplies and mail.

We were able to be with our husbands at least some of every day, to take meals with them and so forth. Halfway across the Atlantic, Paul and I were together for breakfast and he said, "You know what, the ship has stopped!" He said, "I was shaving and the moon was moving around in the porthole. We're turning around," he said.

Sure enough, we were turning around. The *General Edwin D. Patrick* was being positioned next to another ship. A woman on board was suffering from acute appendicitis and their ship had no medical facilities.

I knew what appendicitis felt like, as it had happened once to me. At the time, my sister took me from hospital to hospital. Nobody could take me, because they were all filled with casualties from the war, so by the time I saw a doctor, the pain had subsided.

He said, "If you ever experience that pain again, do not walk, run to the nearest hospital, because it can rupture." So I knew it could be quite serious.

The crew proceeded to execute a very complicated maneuver involving signal lights, pulleys and a basket to transfer the woman to our ship. And after

CHAPTER SEVEN

all that, her pain, too, had subsided. The whole idea of being transferred from one ship to the other was so terrifying to her, she simply refused.

The crossing took nine or ten days. At each meal we always had the same waiter. He was a wonderful waiter. I said to my husband, "I sure like that man. He is so kind and helpful. Let's give him a big tip when we get off the ship in New York."

And my husband said, "You know, Gerda, he is Jewish."

I was very surprised and said, "That nice man is Jewish?!" because we were so programmed to hate Jewish people, you know. I tell you, prejudice is an insidious thing. This was just the first of many experiences that opened my eyes to recognize how brainwashed the people of Germany had become.

We were all very happy when the ship docked in New York City. It was July 16th — my twenty-fourth birthday.

Paul and Gerda "fresh off the boat" in New York City

The first person off the ship was a member of the crew in his dress whites. He fell ignominiously off the gangplank into the harbor! I remember how comical it was to see his little sailor cap floating on the water. I'm sure he didn't think it was funny at all!

The busses were there to pick us up and drive us to the barracks, but nobody stayed in the barracks. We all went to the hotels, because we were all newlyweds.

In the morning, as we got ready to leave the hotel room, I started pulling up the sheets and covers on the bed. My husband laughed at me and said, "What are you doing?"

I said, "I'm making the bed." Because that's what I'd always done!

You recall I mentioned that my grandfather's brother lived in America — Uncle Mathieu? When he found out I was coming to the States, he wrote to me and said, "Why don't you stay with us while Paul is being discharged?" The process of mustering out would take about a week.

Paul took me to Philadelphia by train, and as we got off I wondered how Uncle Mathieu would know me? He hadn't seen me since I was a kid. But then he walked right up to me!

"You must be Gerda," he said.

I spent a week with him and his wife, Agnes, in Philadelphia. They were such wonderful people. Uncle Mathieu played cello with the Philharmonic Orchestra, and he also taught music to young children.

They showed me around the city and treated me royally while I was there. In the morning they served

CHAPTER SEVEN

Lennartz' home in Philadelphia

Uncle Mathieu and Aunt Agnes Lennartz welcome Gerda

grapefruit with breakfast. I'd never even heard of grapefruit. My aunt took me shopping, and I bought a lovely dress for the upcoming trip to Portland.

When Paul was finally free to go, we boarded a train headed west. An hour or so into the trip I asked, "Are we almost there?" because I didn't realize how far away we were from Portland.

I still remember how stunned I was at how vast the expanses were between cities. There were miles and miles of nothing but open fields and hills and valleys devoid of civilization. This was so foreign to me. In Germany you can't go anywhere without seeing homes and villages.

I was awfully sick on the train, just as I'd been on the ship. A sympathetic stewardess finally said, "Here, Honey, eat some of these saltine crackers."

Once in a while a friendly passenger would ask, "Where are you going?" When they heard my answer—Portland, Oregon—they would say, "Oh! You poor girl! It rains there all the time!" I thought, oh, no, where am I going? It was funny.

We travelled from one coast of the United States almost all the way to the other. When the train arrived at the station, Paul pointed through the window and exclaimed, "There's my mother!"

"That's your mother?" I asked incredulously? I don't know what I was expecting, but it certainly wasn't this colorfully-dressed woman with the red nails and green high heels! Bessie McMillan looked my age and I looked hers!

She drew me to her in a warm, welcoming embrace. Tears welled in my eyes. It was like coming

CHAPTER SEVEN

1948 Bessie and Jasper McMillan

home, at last. She was so happy to have a daughter, and I was so happy to have someone I could call "Mom" — and mean it! Even before she'd met me, she'd been so generous, sending me clothes and anything else I needed.

They loaded us and our luggage into their beautiful Pontiac, and we went to their gorgeous house on Flanders Street. The house is still there. The lot next door was theirs, too, and Grandma had developed it into a well-groomed, park-like setting. My husband showed me a picture, later, that was taken when he was home between his first tour of duty and the second. It's of him and his mother sitting on the bench there in that "park".

I said, "What's she talking to you about that she looks so serious?"

Well, he had just told her that he was going to marry a German girl, and at that time, it still wasn't permitted.

I said, "Well, what did she say to that?"

He told me that she said, "Paul, there are good and bad people in every country." She was a wonderful woman and she accepted me into their family without reservation.

Paul telling his mom he's going to marry Gerda

CHAPTER SEVEN

Bessie and Jasper's house on Flanders Street

At the head of a gorgeous stairway, the entire top floor of the house had been prepared for us as a completely self-contained apartment. It was all hardwood floors. Beautiful! We had our privacy, but when Paul was gone during the day, I was able to spend time in his mother's company. She taught me so much, and we had such fun together!

Chapter Eight

Paul's consuming passion was trains. He loved them! No doubt this stemmed partly from the fact that his father, Jasper Alexander McMillan, was a locomotive engineer. When he was a little boy, playing trains with his cousins, if Paul wasn't the engineer, he wouldn't play. He was always in charge, just like he was when he was the head of the motor pool in the Army, but he was always nice, too; people loved him. They called him "Mac".

Before the war, Paul had worked as a mechanic for the Southern Pacific Railroad. When he volunteered for duty, they guaranteed him a job in a position at the same level he'd attained before he went into the Army, so right away he had a job to step into. They made him foreman at the Spokane-Portland-Seattle roundhouse.

The sickness I'd felt on the ship, and then again on the train, continued to plague me. I had expected

CHAPTER EIGHT

it would go away once the travelling was over. When it didn't, I finally went to the doctor.

I said, "Doctor, I throw up every morning."

He said, "Yeah, you are pregnant."

I didn't know that word. I said, "What is 'pregnant'?"

"You are with child!"

"Oh!" So that explained it.

I settled into my role as Paul's wife — soon to be the mother of his child. It is fortunate that when the pain in my side began I quickly recognized it for what it was — my appendix! The words of the doctor back in Germany echoed in my ears: "If you ever experience that pain again, do not walk, *run* to the nearest hospital, because it can rupture."

They took me to the Seventh Day Adventist hospital on Mount Tabor, and my appendix was removed. It was a delicate surgery, because I was four months pregnant, but when it was over Paul wrote to my parents — his German wasn't perfect:

Gerda had an operation. The baby in the stomach is still alive.

The first thing I asked for after the surgery, when my husband came to visit me — I said, "Bring me some liver sausage!"

And the doctor said, "Bring her anything she wants!"

It still bothered me that Paul and I had not been married in the Church. He had promised that we would have a true wedding when we got to the States, so I asked him if we could arrange to have the ceremony.

He had spent six weeks in Germany going through the process to become a Catholic. We had all the papers to prove it, but after a long conversation with the priest in Portland, Paul told me they wouldn't perform the ceremony.

I hadn't understood most of the conversation between Paul and the priest because my English still wasn't very good. I was confused. Why wouldn't he perform the ceremony? But I never got a clear answer, at the time, and there was nothing I could do about it.

CHAPTER EIGHT

My father-in-law would always take me grocery shopping, because Paul was working, and I hadn't yet learned to drive. He would take me in and introduce me as his new daughter-in-law.

I was nervous and afraid, and I said to him, "I don't know what to say when they ask me 'How are you?'"

He said, "Fine, thank you."

I stuck my chin out and said—this was the German in me—"What if I don't *feel* good?"

He repeated slowly and evenly, "You say, 'Fine, thank you!'"

1948 Broadway in downtown Portland

That first month or two, I would go shopping in Portland at Meier and Frank—it was the biggest store; it has since been purchased by Macy's—and I would go home and cry. And why did I cry? You know, when you live in a place for a long time you often run into people you know. But in Portland I looked and looked and looked and never saw a familiar face.

That's why I was so excited, one day, when we were driving down Glisan Street toward downtown, and I spotted a woman I recognized walking along the sidewalk. I said, "Pop! Stop, stop!"

He said, "What for?"

I said, "There's a girl from Germany!"

Can you imagine! And he stopped. I've forgotten her name, now. She was a war bride, too, who had come over on the same ship with me. I couldn't believe it! All the way from Germany; all the way across the United States and here we were both in the same place at the same time. Of course we talked about our trip and so forth, but then she moved to the coast and I never saw her again.

If you move somewhere when you are very young, you fit in quickly, but I came here when I was twenty-four years old, and I had all my basics from Germany. To this day I cannot shake my accent. So people sometimes think I just came off the boat!

I really, really, try hard to speak correctly. One time, a neighbor — she was a very beautiful and talented lady — said "Gerda, you have a fabulous vocabulary."

I thought that was such high praise, especially coming from her. I came home, though, and asked Paul, "What's 'vocabulary'?" To this day, I just never want to speak a word I can't spell. And the spelling here is so different from the way the words sound.

Chapter Eight

I remember vividly, the first three months I was thinking in German, then speaking in English. Then one day I realized, "You know what, I'm thinking in English!" My thinking and speaking had come together.

I was terribly homesick — for many years, really. I didn't like anything here, and nobody could understand that. They would all say, "Oh, how do you like America?" Well, I couldn't say, "I don't like it". Oh, you like it if you come to visit, but if you have to stay for the rest of your life and you don't know if you'll ever go home again to see your loved ones, that is a different story. You have to learn to like it.

It didn't help, either, that I received a letter from my friend, Marichen. She wrote:

> *Guess who dropped by the other day? Gustav! Yes, he was here asking about you. I told him you got married and went to America.*

She told me that he understood, but my heart squeezed a little. So much had happened since we'd been together. I was very glad to hear that Gustl was alive and well, but my future was with Paul, now.

I couldn't go through the rest of my life unsettled and unhappy. I had to learn to like my new home. I was so lucky to have such terrific parents-in-law; they made it so much less difficult.

Grandma offered to buy us our first set of china. I bypassed Meier and Frank and went right to the fanciest china shop. I picked out dishes.

She said, "Oh, Gerda, we're not that kind of people!"

I thought, well, what kind are we? But she agreed to another set, which I have to this day. It's beautiful; gold rimmed. She called it "spode". To me they were just dishes.

When Paul, Jr. was born, in 1949, we went to buy a baby carriage. I found one I liked and Grandma looked at it, because she usually paid for everything.

Chapter Eight

She said, again, "Oh, Gerda, we're not that kind of people."

It was a fancy pram, like they have in Europe, like the Princess would have in England. Well, she didn't think that was for us, so I didn't get that, but I had a very cute one.

My experiences during the bombings in Germany had left me with some shell shock, and so one day when the whole house shook, I ran down to my mother-in-law and exclaimed, "Mom, Mom! Your furnace blew up!" They had this huge, monstrous furnace in the basement, and it always made so much noise, that it was my first thought.

She said, "No Gerda, we had an earthquake."

Now I was really scared, and I had forgotten to bring the baby!

"I'll go get little Paul," she said.

She was the greatest woman. She was, absolutely! God sent me to her.

When my little Paul was two years old, Grandma said — now she'd become Grandma — "You kids should have a house."

We looked around a little at property, but then Paul and I said to each other, "Oh, well, Mom and Dad are over seventy; they won't live that much longer. We will wait and save our money. Someday, we will move into a little house."

The truth was that Grandma wanted to get out of that big house and move into something smaller.

We ended up buying property at 202 SE 86th Avenue in Portland and built a house on it. They gave me all these plans to look at. I mean, I had no idea about houses, or anything, but they gave me these plans. I pointed at one and said, "I want this house!"

Grandma said, "But, Gerda, wouldn't you like to have maybe more this and that?"

"No, no! I want that house!"

And sure enough, we had the house built, with a beautiful round breakfast nook. It's still there, by the way. The house still looks beautiful today, and all the trees we planted sixty years ago — they're still there, now fully grown.

1950 First house, on 86th Street in Portland

Grandma and Grandpa sold the big house. They couldn't find property, but there was a lovely house right across the street from the house we built. So they bought it.

We lived there for a couple of years. And I learned from that experience what I did and didn't want in a house!

Paul was promoted to supervisor in about 1951. His new position was in Vancouver, Washington.

CHAPTER EIGHT

1951 Jasper and Bessie McMillan with Paul, Jr.

"Oh, let's go look for property!" we said. By that time I was more Americanized, and I missed having a dining room; I missed having an entrance hall. I never expected to have a second chance to build a house, especially so soon after we'd built the one we were in, but it came. We found this lot, here, overlooking the rail yard. It was the last one left in the subdivision.

Perhaps we looked too young and maybe we didn't look rich enough. I remember the owner of the property saying, "Oh, but we want a nice house built there."

I thought, oh well, who are we? We had already built a nice house! In the end, she agreed to sell us the property. As soon as we saved enough money, we would build our new home.

Well, Grandma and Grandpa loved driving around looking at houses, so one day they came back and said, "Guess what! We bought the property across the street from yours!" They started building before we did!

When we finally built the house I live in now, the plans were drawn up and then Paul built a model of it for me so I could really see what we would be getting. It was a carefully crafted scale model, complete with furniture I could move around to see how things would fit inside. It was perfect!

In Germany, most everything is red brick or stucco, because they don't have the forests like we have here. When I first came here, I knocked on the wall, and said, "They're all just like wood! Nothing!" As they were building this house, I kept saying, "Oh, gosh, you know, is that strong enough?"

The man building it said, "Gerda, this house will be here when you are gone."

After we moved in, I always used to sing, "I found my thrill on Vancouver hill." And that's absolutely true. I love this house and the fantastic view.

Chapter Nine

I'll bet I knew more about American history than most Americans by the time I finally took my oath of citizenship, in 1951. The courthouse in Portland was crowded. One hundred ninety-eight of us proudly swore our allegiance to the flag of the United States of America.

By this time, my English was much better, so when I ran across some papers one day, I took a moment to try to read them. I thought, hmmm, who is this woman whose last name is McMillan? And, like always, I just went across the street to see my mother-in-law.

"Who is this woman?" I asked.

"Oh, I knew he should have told you he was married before!"

He'd been married to her! He had never told me. My mind flew back to the day that little boy outside the boxcars had informed me that Paul was married. Paul should have told me the truth then. Apparently, they were going through a divorce at that time, and Paul probably thought I would never find out. He probably realized I would never come with him, if I did find out, because I was strict Catholic.

Paul knew explicitly that we would never be allowed to marry in the Catholic Church.

If I had been able to read English at the time, I would have seen references to Paul's previous marriage in the marriage application papers. The "marriage investigation" letter that was issued by the U.S. military before we left Germany also clearly stated, "both have expressed the intention to renounce the Catholic faith and enter a Protestant church".

I would never have agreed to that!

They have a saying in Germany, "There is nothing so fine-spun that does not come out in the light of the sun." Don't keep secrets. Just let them come out, because later on it could cause disappointment.

Chapter Nine

Now I knew why we had to get married by a Justice of the Peace in Germany and why the Catholic priest in Portland wouldn't agree to marry us. In those days, if you were divorced, you could not marry again in the Catholic Church.

These revelations left me with a sense of betrayal, but what was I going to do? I couldn't run home to Mama.

I was a churchgoer at the time. Paul could take it, but mostly leave it, and he usually fell asleep during the sermon, which was embarrassing to me.

A woman I became friends with went to the Methodist Church. She took me under her wing and got me going to her church from then on.

I thought, well, if they don't want to marry me in the Catholic Church, I believe in God and God is everywhere, whatever the church.

So I went to the Methodist Church.

This same woman got me involved in things and one time she said, "You have to come to the Sunday school. I'll introduce you to the children and you can read to them this little story." So I read the little story and the children all just stared at me.

Finally, one of them said, "She talks funny!"

When they had an open house, the children's parents came to see what their children had been doing in Sunday school. That same child said to his parents, "Here's my teacher!"

And I thought, Oh my Gosh, I can hardly speak English well, let alone be considered his teacher!

But the little kids were so sweet.

My father came to see me in America. At the time he came — it was around 1953 — they didn't have jets. He came on a twin-prop plane from Germany to New York, and from New York he took another flight to Portland.

When he got off the plane, he said, "This must be the ends of the earth!" because it was such a long trip.

My little Paul was just maybe four years old, and he had to share a room with my father. Shortly after they went to bed the first night, Paul comes out, "Me is afraid of the big boy, Mom."

I said, "Well, Honey, it's your grandpa, you know — your *Opa*." It was because his grandpa was wearing a long dressing gown, like Scrooge wore!

He stayed with us three months. In early spring, my husband took us on a trip by car to Crater Lake. I tell you, the road up to Crater Lake, on both sides you couldn't see anything but snow. We stopped once along the way to take pictures, then got back in the car and continued on.

About half a mile up the road towards the lake, my father said, "Oh, I left my glasses!" He had put them on the trunk and they'd fallen off. We went back and, sure enough, there they were lying in the snow.

We stayed in cabins at the lake, and I'm such a city girl. All I could think of at night when I heard a little rustling was, Oh my Gosh, I think there are mice in here! I'm sure there were. Luckily, I never saw one, but I could hear them!

Chapter Nine

1953 Josef Velten

I got my first opportunity to return to Germany in 1955. Grandma agreed to go with me and little Paul.

Grandma was probably sixty-eight years old at the time. She said, "Gerda, I will go with you, but I won't stay with your parents. I will stay in a hotel nearby."

I decided Paul and I would stay in the hotel, as well, because my parents' apartment was very small.

When my father discovered I wouldn't be staying with them, the first thing he said was, "Oh, it's not good enough for you to be with us at home?"

To some extent, he was right: they didn't have their own bathroom! I was, by this time, spoiled by American standards. But the main reason, really, was that Grandma needed me, because she could not speak German.

We travelled about five days by train from Portland to New York City and spent the night at the Taft Hotel. Paul, Jr. was quite taken with the young ladies, dressed in short-skirted uniforms, who were always on hand with their little trays, selling tiny cakes they called honey buns.

From there, we boarded the luxurious ocean liner, *SS America*. Built in 1939, this great ship was once known as "the queen" of the U.S. Merchant Marines. She was seven hundred twenty-two feet long and ninety-three feet wide. During World War II, she was renamed the *USS Westpoint* and served as a troop transport ship, returning to her original purpose, and name, when the war was over.

We were fortunate to sail on her during her glory days. She was retired from service in 1964. After that,

Chapter Nine

SS America

1955 Bessie, Paul Jr., Gerda in the ship's dining room

she was sold many times. In 1993, she was sold one last time. While crossing the Atlantic under tow, the tow line broke during a storm. Crew tried to reattach the line, but were not successful. Ultimately, she was abandoned at sea and finally grounded off the Canary Islands, where she eventually broke up and sank. Quite a sorrowful ending for such a beautiful ship.

It took about eight or nine days to get to Bremerhaven. Paul, Jr. thought the whole thing was a grand adventure. We were returning to our stateroom one afternoon, and he went running ahead of Grandma and me. When we got to the room we found he'd donned his life jacket. He was ready to "man the life boats"!

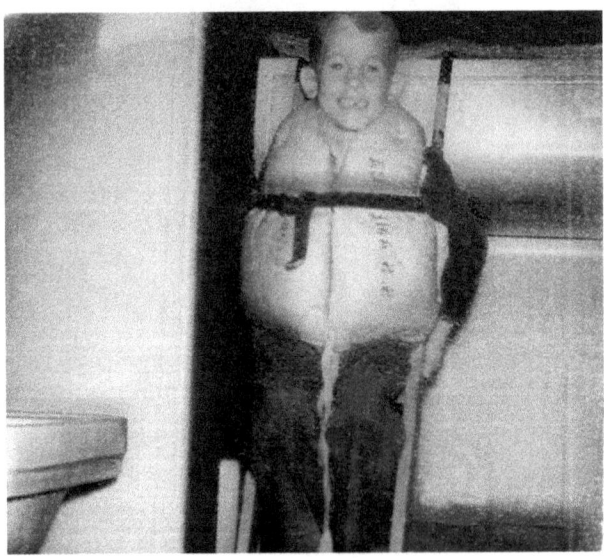

Paul, Jr. ready to "man the life boats"

CHAPTER NINE

After a few hours layover, we went on by train to Bonn.

Upon our arrival, Christel presented her three sons. She'd had another son after Heinz returned from the war. His name was Paul, too, named after my husband.

Little Hans, her oldest boy, must have been about eight or nine years old. He bowed in front of Grandma and clicked his heels.

She was so impressed. "Oh, what a polite boy!" she exclaimed!

But Jup — ah, he was still my favorite!

My stepbrother, Willy, and his wife, Katherine (they called her Däddy) had built a mansion sometime after I left Germany. He had done very well in the *markthalle*.

Däddy was not too fond of me, because I had married an American soldier, you know — I had married the enemy. But when she saw me, she said, "You sure look well taken care of."

And I thought, you betcha, I do! Because I had all these clothes and everything money could buy.

Bonn had not changed. I had changed. I definitely had changed. And they let me know.

They said, "You know, we could listen to you for hours," because I now had an accent with my German, just like I had here with my English. And they loved hearing me talk. *Ja*! I just didn't fit in anywhere!

We stayed in Germany for a month.

Poor Grandma! She was by herself in the hotel much of the time, because she didn't want to go, go, go every day like my sister and I did.

She would say, "No, Gerda, I will stay here. You just go."

She stayed in her room a good deal of the time, because whenever she went in or out, she had to pass through the hotel dining room, and people would try to talk to her. She didn't speak any German, so that was uncomfortable for her.

In Germany, whatever the weather, they turn off the central heating system in May. She caught pneumonia while we were there.

I called the doctor. The doctor came to the hotel.

When he was finished examining her, he took me out into the hallway and he said, "I tell you, your mother-in-law won't have very much longer to live. She has a bad heart."

Oh! She lived seventeen years after that! So much for the German doctors!

Christel and Heinz lived in Beuel, so we visited with them there on several occasions while we were in Germany. In those days, when people lived outside of the city, they had no bathrooms — they had just little outhouses. I had such a problem with Paul, Jr. When he had to go, he didn't want to go into the outhouse. It was so gross! But, of course, there was no choice.

I said, "Just back into it!"

During one of these visits, the church bells started ringing. My heart leapt, and I was immediately transported back in time to my little apartment above the bakery in Bonn and the joyous clamoring of the bells.

"Oh, Christel!" I exclaimed. "Open the windows so I can hear those bells!"

Chapter Nine

One day, there was a religious procession in Beuel. Of course they can't go down every street, but Christel, in her usual assertive fashion, went out and pleaded with them.

"My sister is here from America. Would you come through my street?"

The band and the whole procession diverted down her street for our enjoyment! I had to hand it to her: she wasn't afraid to ask for what she wanted.

On Mother's day, I said to her, "Let's go visit Mom's grave."

Christel said, "There is no grave."

This came as a shock to me. I said, "What?"

She said, "No, after so many years, if the children don't renew the plot, they take them out."

Ja! That's what happens! That was a big shock to me. The grave was no longer there, because they don't have the space like they do here.

My husband used to tell me, "You know, all of Germany is no bigger than the state of Oregon."

And can you imagine the number of people there, compared to here? Over eighty million there and somewhat less than four million here. It was totally different, you know; really different. There, if the graves aren't maintained, they are used again.

Grandma and I and Paul, Jr. took a little side trip to *Köln* one day. We were waiting in *Köln* for the train back to Bonn. When the next one came in, the man who was driving it came out. He recognized me! It was Willy, the one who tried to kiss me in the stairway in Bonn. After all these years!

Chapter Ten

Josef Velten, my father, died of cancer in 1960. Time was short between diagnosis and death.

I told him I was going to get there to see him, and he told everyone in the hospital his daughter was coming from America — but things did not go according to plan: there wasn't enough time to apply for and get a visa.

My stepbrother, Willy, told me, "Gerda, it wouldn't do any good to come here to see your father, because he is so at the end, and it is very cold here."

The *Rhein* was frozen. I was so sad and wracked with guilt — for the next two years I struggled with it and cried often. It felt like I'd let him down.

Willy died just a few years later.

When Christel gave me the news, she said, "Ah, Gerda, when we went to visit him in the hospital, you could hear him yell, '*Das kann nicht sein!*' (This cannot be!)"

Chapter Ten

He knew he was dying, but he couldn't believe it, because he was only fifty years old.

I didn't get back to Germany again until the summer of 1966. I wanted to go see my family and so my husband said, "Well, go with Junior. I don't want to go."

Paul, Jr. invited his friend John, who lived in the neighborhood, to go with us. The three of us went to Germany. The boys were seventeen years old, and they were able to go everywhere without me. They were having a great time.

But I had a sixth sense that there was something not right here at home. We had reservations to stay for a month, but when I called home in the middle of the night and my husband wasn't home, the boys and I went the next day to change our reservations to go home sooner. I called Paul to let him know.

He wasn't at the airport when we arrived, which would never have happened before. A taxi delivered us to the house. Paul came home maybe half an hour later, and I confronted him.

"Where were you?" I knew something was definitely wrong, and that's when he told me he was with another woman.

I nearly fainted!

Right there, in that moment, my illusions were shattered. It was devastating! The whole foundation of my life shifted that day. My fairy tale life had taken a Grimm turn, and the unquestioning faith I'd had in my husband was gone. Our relationship had suffered a tremendous blow.

After the initial shock, I thought, no woman is taking over my life!

Not for a moment did I consider stepping aside, walking away. Why would I just roll over and let another woman take my husband from me? And the prospect of breaking up our family, of putting Paul, Jr. in that position, was completely abhorrent to me.

When you have a marriage in trouble, like ours was, both people have to be willing to work at it, to make it right. In our case, neither of us wanted to end the marriage.

While Paul made some changes, not all of the responsibility for how it had come to this could be assigned to him. I found out where I was wrong, too, but it would be much later before I fully understood the underlying root of the problem.

Grandma and Grandpa had always told me, "Gerda, you don't have to go to work."

But I had always wanted to do something besides stay at home, so when this happened I went looking for a job. Under the circumstances, I really needed to, to keep my sanity.

There was an opening at Hickory Farms in the mall. I went and applied because I knew all the cheeses from Germany, Holland, and Sweden. I thought well, maybe they can use me.

So I applied and they said, "We'll call you."

But I never received a call.

Then there was a notice in the paper that a major department store was opening in the mall on Hayden Island.

Chapter Ten

The manager asked me, "Gerda, why do you want to work?" because it was obvious I didn't need the money.

It was simple: I needed to do it for myself. My "self", whom I'd given up almost entirely in my misguided concept of what it took to be a good wife. Cooking and cleaning and taking care of Paul and our son — all very important, but it didn't do much to keep me interesting. Paul was out there in the world every day, meeting interesting people — interesting women.

They hired me and several others. We trained for four days and then the store opened and we were on. But at the end of the training, I went down to the lady who trained us and I told her, "You know what, I really enjoyed all of it, but most of it went over my head, so thank you very much."

She said, "Gerda, you be here on opening day at such and such time." And that was the best thing that could have happened to me.

They put me in the children's department, and people just loved me! I met many, many people. I still have friends from that time.

Paul and I started taking time to get away together and have time to ourselves, to re-invent our relationship, because we didn't choose to give up on the life that we'd built together.

Don't be that housewife, because that's the biggest mistake you'll make. I was just the housewife type. I was always in a dress, but never any make-up. You can be a housewife, but make efforts to look nice when he comes home, because they are out there with all these good-looking women dressed up to work, and then he comes home to this nothing. But when I went to work — boy! It was a different story! I always had his respect, but I got more because now I was bringing home a paycheck.

In time, I had the opportunity to work in any and all of the departments at the store. I was very good at sales. My advice to women shoppers: "Wear your blouse tight enough to show you are a woman and loose enough to show that you are a lady."

The best of the sales staff were invited to go to the Seattle market on buying trips, all expenses paid. That was me. What fun that was! I also got to do some modeling for the store and my picture was used in some advertising.

In fact, I was such a good salesperson, a lady came into the store one day, and when she saw me she looked a little panicked and warned me to stay away from her, because she never left the store without buying something from me!

But I enjoyed working in the men's department the most. Oh, women do a lot of shopping, alright; they often try on everything in the store…and then walk out with nothing! But men! When they come in, they're only interested in quickly finding what they need; they buy it and off they go!

Yes, working in the store did a lot for my self-esteem, and things between Paul and I were getting better.

One time, we had a snow storm. I and my co-workers had just closed up the store and everyone had filtered out of the parking lot. I got into my car,

CHAPTER TEN

dreading the drive home. There was a sharp rap on the window. It was Paul. He'd walked all the way from our house, crossing the bridge over the river, just because he knew I would be anxious about the drive home!

ᇮ

My cousin Gertrud and her boyfriend, Kurt, worked at the famous Hotel Petersberg. It was a palatial hotel high on a hill on the east bank of the *Rhein* overlooking the cities of Bonn and Königswinter. British Prime Minister Neville Chamberlain stayed there in 1938 when he met with Hitler in an attempt to avert war. After the war, the Allied High Commission took it over, until the Federal Republic of Germany (West Germany) became a sovereign state in 1955.

Gertrud and I used to write back and forth. She wanted very much to come to America.

The prospect of having her here was so exciting to me, I said, "Well, why don't you come?"

When her parents died — my Uncle Adam and Aunt Gertrud — their various properties were divided between Gertrud and Ulrich. Ulrich had done very well for himself, working for Chancellor Adenauer. He was in charge of the extensive grounds surrounding the Chancellor's home. When Adenauer died, the family gave Ulrich one of the valuable paintings from the estate to thank him for all his years of service.

Gertrud wasn't quite so well off, but she sold her property, so there was a little money to help fund the move.

Of course, it wasn't as easy as just deciding to come to America; they could only come if they had a sponsor and jobs waiting for them. Paul was skeptical, at first, but he finally agreed to sponsor them. I got Gertrud a job as a housekeeper and Kurt found a job, as well.

Grandma fixed up the basement for them, so Gertrud and Kurt were able to live there, until they were able to buy their own home.

ೞ

The Korean War had come and gone. I'd felt little direct impact from it. But Paul, Jr. was drafted into the Army during the Vietnam War, during the first round in 1969. I was so worried that he would be sent into the fighting!

I said, "How terrible! I have had enough of war! Now my son may have to go to Vietnam and maybe get killed!"

My father-in-law wrote to Olympia about how Junior was the only grandson holding the name McMillan. He didn't want that jeopardized.

Apparently that had some effect, because guess where they sent him? To Germany! He was with what the German's called the Panzer division. Tanks! And still I worried sick. When he flew over to Germany and they put the tanks into the airplane, I fretted,

Chapter Ten

"How can it possibly stay in the air with the weight of all those soldiers and tanks!"

While Junior was away, I said to Grandma, "Grandma, there is this beautiful property in the corner of our subdivision..." She went and bought it for him!

On April 28, 1972 Jasper ran across the street from his house and burst into ours. He said, "You'd better come. I think there's something wrong with Grandma!"

We found her collapsed on the floor in her bathroom. Every night she performed the usual feminine ritual of removing her make-up before bed. On this particular night, she suffered a heart attack and died instantly. We knew she was dead as soon as we saw her.

Jasper was devastated. He'd met Bessie Champagne in 1908. As an engineer for Southern Pacific Railroad, his route took him from Portland to Roseburg, where he would spend the night before doing the return trip. Bessie lived in Roseburg. They were married there on the ninth of November, 1909.

There was never anyone else for Jasper. He could see only Bessie. In fact, he hadn't been real keen on having children. He'd once seen a woman in childbirth, and that had made up his mind on the subject. He didn't want Bessie to go through that. Bessie had other ideas, although Paul was an only child. Perhaps she agreed with Jasper after that!

Her hobby was quilt-making, and she was very good at it. The last one she made has never been used.

I've kept it all these years and will give it to Valisha — a gift from her great-grandma.

As Jasper got on in years, macular degeneration rendered him legally blind. Bessie didn't drive, but she did keep Jasper going, even though he probably shouldn't have been driving. I can still hear her saying, "Daddy, you can do this!" And off they'd go!

Bessie was buried in Portland, at Lincoln Memorial Park, on Mount Scott. Jasper stood at the graveside long after everyone else had gone. Finally, I heard him say, "Bessie, I won't be long."

Jasper stayed in their house across the street. Whether I was ready to cook dinner or not, he would come across every night for dinner, all dressed up, and he would sit in the breakfast nook and wait. He died just eight months later and was laid to rest next to Bessie, at the cemetery on Mount Scott.

When Paul, Jr. got out of the military and came home, he met a girl and got married. Paul and I decided to give Junior Grandma and Grandpa's house, which had been left to us and was all paid for. He and Nancy sold it and used the money to build their new home on the piece of land his grandparents had bought for him. Junior doesn't live in the house any longer. I have great neighbors who live there now, but I called the house the Titanic, because it has those stacks on the roof, like smokestacks.

Chapter Eleven

My sister called one night.

"How would you like to have Heinz and me come to visit?"

Oh, I was in heaven to hear that!

They bought tickets to fly over, and we were supposed to pick them up at the airport. When the time approached and we were confirming all the information, we discovered their tickets would fly them into Vancouver, alright — Vancouver, Canada! And still we had to go pick them up!

It was amazing to me that Christel was coming by plane at all, because she was deathly afraid of flying, but the Germans are not very kind, sometimes, and over the years her friends had made such fun of her, saying, "Hah! You'll never go."

Finally, she'd had enough and said, "Oh, I'll show 'em!" And that's how my sister came to America.

Arriving victorious, she came off the plane like everything belonged to her — like she was the queen! Oh, yeah!

Anyway, I said to Christel, "We're going to stay in the hotel, because we've been driving already for six hours."

"No hotel! I've been on that plane for all these hours! I want to go directly to your house!"

We knew she had no idea how long the trip would be, but we gave in and drove all the way back to Vancouver, Washington.

During the trip home, she kept saying, "Where is everything, where is everything!" because, like me, she wasn't used to seeing so many unpopulated areas.

When she came into my house for the first time, she exclaimed, "Oh, I like your house!"

She was my older sister — I was quite relieved. Thank goodness! She likes the house!

Christel and Heinz

Chapter Eleven

We drove them all around Portland, giving them the tour. In the Sellwood district, Heinz was looking out the window, really taking it all in. Suddenly, he saw this HOUSE. It was really big and fancy and well-maintained.

He said, "My, that is a beautiful house! It must be a resort!"

I could see he was impressed — Germans like beautiful things.

"Yes," I said, "It's the last one!" It was a funeral home. I'm not sure he thought that was as funny as I did.

After dinner one evening, at the Holland restaurant, Christel and I were standing in the background while the men paid the bill. Another guest from the restaurant approached Christel and looked admiringly at the piece of jade she was wearing. It was a gorgeous piece I had given her years ago. I got it at I. Magnin, which was the top store in Portland at the time, but Christel never believed it was real.

The woman exclaimed, "Oh, what a beautiful piece of jade!"

Of course, Christel had to ask me what she had said, because she didn't understand English. I translated for her and just stood back and smiled, happy that somebody else had told Christel that it was something worthwhile. Now she was proud of it!

Christel wasn't very good with money. She would buy anything, whether she could afford it or not. Now, that's where I draw the line. I never, never bought anything I couldn't afford. I always had to know I had the money to pay for it. But Christel was just the opposite.

My father always said, "I can bring the money through the front door in a wheelbarrow and she will take it right out the back door."

Christel got the right husband. Heinz wore gold cuff-links and he always wore a cravat. He was a painter and restored antique furniture. His skill and reputation were such that he could name his price. He always took Christel shopping at the fanciest stores, and he would sit there while she tried things on and came out to show him: "Heinz, you like this?"

Of course, no trip to the Pacific Northwest would be complete without going to the beach. We made reservations at our favorite place — Salishan Spa and Golf Resort. It's in a beautiful, wooded setting, and we had a kitchen and everything, you know, and she wouldn't stay there.

"No, I'm not going to stay here!"

"Why not?" I was offended!

"If I'm going to the beach, I'm going to be seeing the ocean!"

"Okay," I said and stomped downstairs to the office.

I said, "My sister would like to be closer to the ocean."

And they said, "That's okay, Mrs. McMillan, we'll just credit you for a later time."

We used to go there at least twice a year.

A short distance away, on the ocean side of the street is the Cavalier. It's very beautiful. Okay, we had just put our suitcases in the bedroom and BANG! The

Chapter Eleven

furnace blew up! Really, truthfully! Oh, she wouldn't stay there! Back to Salishan we went.

ଔ

In 1982, my husband and I went to visit Christel and Heinz. The four of us drove to Holland. It was quite an experience.

One of their friends had a condo in Noordwijk-by-the-Sea. When we arrived, we all took turns taking showers. There was no separate stall for the shower. The water fell right onto the floor from a primitive shower head in the ceiling.

But Noordwijk by the sea is beautiful, just beautiful. That's where I bought my wooden shoes and a tulip pin.

We stopped for lunch at a little restaurant one day, and my husband, being American, wanted a ham sandwich. So we ordered it. The server came with half a ham!

Paul said, "No, I just wanted a sandwich."

The waitress said "Yes, sir. You just cut whatever you want."

I asked for asparagus, and they brought me a whole pound of it!

The trip to Holland was all on the autobahn and Heinz was the driver. Paul sat in the front with him, and my sister and I in sat the back. They go like 100 miles an hour on the autobahn — and my husband said afterward, "Do not ever invite me to drive again with Heinz!"

Chapter Twelve

Paul, Jr. and Nancy had one child. Her name is Valisha — in German it would be Valischa. It is such a shame Grandma and Grandpa never got to see her.

Grandpa had always said, "Oh, I would love to have a little red-haired granddaughter."

Valisha has fire-red curls! We love each other, and she's a wonderful granddaughter.

Our son and his wife got a divorce when Valisha was still very young. Nancy remarried. Once in a while, I would pick up Valisha and keep her for a day or so. Divorce is so hard on children, no matter what anyone else will tell you. And if you're the grandparents on the father's side, you just get to see your grandchildren once in a while, on holidays.

My granddaughter has taken some nice trips with me. You know, everything I did was not just ordinary.

I told my friends, "I'm taking my granddaughter to the zoo."

Chapter Twelve

They said, "How nice", but what they didn't know was which zoo: it was in San Diego!

For both of us, that was our first airplane ride. We took off from Portland, and as the plane climbed up into the clouds, Valisha looked at me and she said, "Grandma, is this where God is?"

We stayed in Vacation Village, close to the ocean in San Diego, and she fell in love with a little duckling.

Oh my Gosh, she loved animals — and I'm just the opposite! In fact, one time she came to our house carrying a little box.

I said, "What do you have in the box?"

"Oh, Grandma, I've got this cute mouse!"

"Oh!" I exclaimed in alarm. "Take this thing out of here!" you know, and she cried. I said, "Out, out!"

And she said, "In the garage?"

"For heaven's sake," I said, "not in the garage!" because where I was from we wouldn't have anything crawling around.

We had these lovely neighbors in the first house we had built — Dana was the woman's name — and, *ja*, there was a mouse in the garage!

I went outside and called out to her, "Oh, Dana, there's a mouse in the garage!"

Oh, well, she just came with a broom. I would have given the mouse the house!

Remember my mother's saying, "If it crawls, step on it!" I got my fear from her.

My granddaughter was raised by her mother, who loves animals. They lived in the country, and they had horses. So I went to pick up Valisha one time.

She was about six or seven years old, at the time, and she said, "Grandma, come and see Forrest."

It was the horse.

I said, "I see Forrest from here."

She said, "Come on Grandma, pet Forrest."

I said, "No, no. I see Forrest is a very nice horse." Scared to death of the horse!

Paul loved dogs. The first time we got a puppy, we went to the pound and adopted one.

When we got in the car, Paul said, "Here, hold the puppy."

I said, "No. I can't." I just couldn't touch it.

Paul was wearing a leather jacket, so he tucked the puppy inside his coat so he could use both hands to drive.

Later, we always had a dog. Usually, it was a Saint Bernard. One time, Paul and I were walking our burly guy when a policeman came along.

"What do you feed that guy!" He exclaimed, because it was a really big dog.

Paul shot back, "Policemen's ankles!" Oh, I would have been terrified to talk to a policemen that way. But not Paul!

଄

Paul and I took Valisha with us to Germany when she was ten years old. Unlike her grandfather, Valisha was delighted with the high-speed autobahn.

"Why can't they drive this fast back home?" she exclaimed!

CHAPTERTWELVE

It was such fun introducing our granddaughter to the home I loved.

One of the high points of that trip was a visit to the *Drachenfels* (Dragon's Rock) and the fortress ruins there. Inside a cave on this mountain is where legend says Siegfried dispatched the fearsome dragon, Fafnir.

The fortress was built between 1136 and 1167. Not much of the ancient, crumbling edifice remains, but its state of decay just adds to the romance and mystery

The Drachenfels

of the place. You can reach the top on foot, by rail, or by donkey. Not surprisingly, Valisha wanted to ride the donkey.

Valisha on the donkey ride up to the Drachenfels

Later, we walked along the *Rhein* and stopped to eat at my favorite restaurant, Im Bären. The memories were vivid, there, of my parents and those simpler times we shared while they were both alive. Retracing those steps with Valisha was the closest I could come to having her meet them, and I knew they would have loved her dearly.

And she loved Germany! We were waiting at a crosswalk one day. Paul was holding her hand on one side and I was on the other.

Chapter Twelve

Suddenly, she looked up at us and said, "I don't know about you guys, but I'd come back here, again!" You know, of course, how much that pleased me.

Gerda and Valisha at Christel and Heinz' house

Chapter Thirteen

In 1984, a truly wonderful opportunity came our way. Twenty-three men were being selected as coach attendants to crew a train behind the old 4449 steam-powered engine that Paul had helped refurbish back in 1974.

The last remaining engine of its kind, the famous 4449 steam-powered locomotive had made the run for years between Los Angeles and San Francisco. It was retired in 1956 and donated to the city of Portland in 1958, where it went on stationary display in Oaks Amusement Park until 1974. It was then restored and returned to service for the revival of the American Freedom Train as it toured the United States between 1975 and 1976.

The purpose of this jaunt was to publicize the Louisiana World's Fair in New Orleans. The 4449 was almost completely rebuilt for the occasion, and the entire train was "Daylight-painted" — a term coined to describe the orange, red, silver and black color

CHAPTER THIRTEEN

The 4449 stands ready at Union Station, Portland, Oregon

scheme, which characterized trains during that time period.

Paul was one of those chosen for the honor. For him it was an all-expense-paid trip. We would have to pay my fare. I wasn't real keen on going, but my boss urged me to do it. In the end, I didn't want to disappoint Paul, so I went. And I am so glad I did. The experience made a believer out of me — if you want to truly see the United States, go by rail.

It was a twenty-nine day trip, beginning May 5, 1984. Among those notable persons aboard were Al McCready, retired managing editor of the Oregonian, and his wife, Connie, the former mayor of Portland. In addition to several passengers from the Pacific

Northwest, one passenger was from Switzerland, and many were from the east coast.

Some of the 4449 crew

There were two crew cars, eight coaches, two lounge cars, one VIP car, 416 passengers and twenty-eight crew. Thousands of people turned out to see us off. The Grant High School Band played, and on the Willamette River a fireboat jetted a powerful spray of water into the air in honor of our departure. It was a media extravaganza! The train was overflowing with television crew and other reporters when we left the station.

The engine fired up, sending a plumage of smoke and steam skyward. The wheels started turning and the 4449, capable of exerting 64,800 pounds of tractive effort, put her shoulder into moving the train's ponderous weight. We were officially underway.

CHAPTER THIRTEEN

Cars, planes and helicopters paced us along the freeway between Portland and Salem.

Fireboat send-off

By the time we got to Salem, where the news media crews got off, I was offered a chance to work in the lounge car with Paul. I gladly accepted, because it would give me something to do.

That first day, we headed up into the Cascades with a little boost from a "helper" engine we picked up in Oakridge. The train lumbered up into the snow-covered mountains, around hairpin curves and through tunnel after tunnel. The 4449's mournful "woo, woo" and the breathy panting of her efforts broke the otherwise bucolic silence. That was a really memorable stretch of track.

We got into Klamath Falls at about six o'clock p.m. It seemed like at least one half the population had turned out to greet us!

Because there were no sleeping quarters on the train, it stopped every night and the crew and passengers were accommodated, most often, at a Hyatt Regency Hotel. In Klamath Falls it was high on a hill overlooking the town.

The next morning we resumed our trip and about an hour-and-a-half into it they decided to do a "photo run-by". We would do this every day at about the same time.

During this exercise everyone detrains and stays alongside the track. The train is backed up about a mile before it comes rolling back at full-speed, smoke and steam streaming, sparks flying and the whistle blowing. Lots of video was shot and photographs were taken.

In addition to our other duties, we were also "drafted" to sell souvenirs at each of the stops. This presented a problem for our engineer, Doyle McCormack. How was he going to keep track of us amidst the throngs when it was time for us to leave? How was he going to be sure we had all gotten back aboard? We solved this problem by tying balloons to our shoulders, and right away Al McCready coined a name for us — we were Balloonatics!

I won't go into the rest of the trip in as much detail. The subsequent days were more of the same as we passed through cities like Sacramento, San Francisco, San Antonio, Houston, Dallas and many more. My favorite city was San Antonio, where they

CHAPTER THIRTEEN

4449 photo run-by

"Baloonatics" selling souvenirs

have the river walk, although I was horrified to see the filth and debris that littered the landscape beside the tracks on the outskirts.

Crowds of eager spectators congregated all along the way, even in some of the most unlikely places where the population was sparse — we wondered where they all came from!

Over the course of our month-long adventure we became good friends with the rest of the crew. Evenings would find us dining together, laughing and trading stories of the day.

When we arrived in New Orleans, an enormous crowd greeted us and a band played "When the Saints Go Marching In".

Oh, that was fantastic, I tell you! What memories!

Gerda working in the club car

Chapter Fourteen

The store I worked for changed names several times in the twenty years I worked there. And it was there, in 1985, that I met Frank. Physically, and in many other ways, he reminded me so much of *Herr* Müller, my first love. He lived in the neighborhood and came into the store nearly every day. I think he enjoyed seeing the sales ladies because we all dressed beautifully.

On one of these occasions, I was standing at one of the rounders that held clothing. My hand was resting on top. He reached out and touched my hand, and it was like I was struck by lightning! That was it!

From that time on I tried to work it so I was free to take a break when he came in. We'd go into the mall for coffee.

He drove a tanker truck for a major oil company, but because he was divorced and needed to earn some extra money to pay child support, he also worked part-time washing dishes at a nearby restaurant. It wasn't very upscale, but they had live music in the evenings, so some of my friends and I started going there after work to dance. I always hoped I'd see Frank, but he never came out of the kitchen. Still, I knew he was there. We became such regulars that whenever we walked through the door the band would start playing my favorite song, "New York, New York".

Paul had no problem with me going out dancing after work. He said, "Go, have fun!"

A good friend of mine, who was also from Germany, called one night while I was out.

"Is Gerda home?"

Paul said, "No, she's out with her friends, dancing."

"What!" She was shocked because this was definitely out of character for me.

People who knew me would never imagine that I would go out dancing with friends, because I was always so strict and very "proper". The first day I worked in the children's department, my son came in and he said, "Mom you look like a school teacher."

The restaurant was such a dive, I can't believe I spent so much time there. But my interest in Frank was unrelenting. He was actually pretty shy, and I think he may have been afraid of me, at first.

I didn't stop to think what I wanted out of the deal. In fact, one time he agreed to meet me outside of the store. I picked him up in my car. A few moments after he got in, his hand moved close to mine! That brought me up short!

"I'm married," I said.

Chapter Fourteen

"I'm in a ten-year relationship," said he.

Good, I thought! I just wanted to get to know him better.

Paul and I were coming home from Portland to Vancouver one day, and I saw the tanker truck Frank drove.

I exclaimed, "Oh, there's Frank! That's my friend!"

Paul said, "Oh, that's the man you met that comes to your store?" I had spoken to Paul about him quite openly.

I said, "Yes! He is the neatest man!"

"Well, invite him to come to our house."

So, I did!

My husband was quite the special man. He was sure of himself. He could stand up to anybody because he was very bright, and everybody loved him. Years ago, in Wiesbaden, when he was in charge of the American motor pool, I'd noticed he would always, say "Hi, my friend," or "See you later, my friend."

One day, back then, I asked him, "Why do you call everybody your friend?" But that was just Paul.

Frank came into his life and Paul welcomed him as a friend.

This man became part of our family. Frank was at our house nearly every weekend. I really think he looked up to Paul, seeing him almost as a surrogate father, although Paul was only about thirteen years his senior.

Still, we never really knew much about Frank. He never talked about his past. The present seemed to be all that was relevant to him.

℅

The flag, and all it represents, meant so much to Paul. So one day he sent me shopping while he and Frank worked together to install in our backyard a tall flagpole crowned with an American eagle.

He sent me shopping because he knew I would not agree to have it. Not because I had any objection to the flag, itself, but because the grand display would seem so pretentious, to me.

When I came home, I said, "What's that?"

1993 Frank and Paul raising the flagpole

CHAPTER FOURTEEN

He said, "That's for our flag."

I said, "You're going to have a flag up there? People will think the governor lives up here!" In my mind, only famous or wealthy people would have a flag like that.

The flagpole is so high, it was quite a project, but Paul and Frank managed it together. There is a tiny plaque at the base of it with both their names on it.

When it was finished, our neighbor Glen came over and played taps on his bugle while the flag was being raised for the first time.

Glenn playing taps while the flag is raised

The flagpole with the U.S. colors flying

Chapter Fourteen

☙

Eventually, I retired from working at the department store, but I found I really didn't like being retired, so I got a job in the gift shop at the Doubletree Inn.

I was so taken with Frank, I talked about him all the time. When she'd had all she could take on the subject, the woman who was my boss finally said one day, "Let's take him to the river!"

I wondered what in the world she was talking about!

"Why," I asked?

"Let's see if he can walk on water!"

But that's how completely my world had begun to revolve around Frank.

He was so much a part of our family, I would leave him "to do" lists — chores to do around the house while I was gone. One time I came home to find them all done, and he'd left me a little note:

> *Did it "My Way"* (his favorite song)
> *Vacumed all carpet, dusted and Pledged furniture; cleaned glass-top tables and baseboards; mopped kitchen and hall; swept and washed stairs; swept stoop and front steps; shook pine needles out of Madame's bath rug; swept garage. To Hell with porch and furniture today. Paul and I will do it later, together. Now taking bath on my time and going home. Bye-bye. And yes, vacuum has two U's.*

Like Paul, Frank loved animals, particularly dogs. The neighbor's dog, Sonny, became a routine visitor at our house. He would come around to the back door, looking for Frank, who always had a treat for him. They were pretty good pals.

When I was seventy-one, the gift shop closed, but I still wasn't ready to sit at home doing nothing. I applied at a very high-end clothing store, which was then in Vancouver Mall.

During my interview, the woman said, "We don't have anything right now."

I had just barely walked in the door at home when the phone rang.

She said, "Gerda, I think we have someplace for you. Please come in again."

When I got there she said, "Yes, we can give you the line of Elizabeth Arden cosmetics."

I was well-dressed and well-groomed, but I knew nothing about cosmetics. So I said to my granddaughter, who at that time was twenty-one or twenty-two, "Honey, would you come at night" — I worked at night at the store — "so I can practice on you doing makeovers?"

She came, and she would teach me, because she was very crafty.

I loved working there. The discount was a nice perk. It was a good job, and I got pretty good at it. Cash registers had become more like computers, by this time, so I was still learning new things.

After a year-and-a-half, or maybe two, they took Elizabeth Arden out of all the stores. By that time, I was seventy-two or seventy-three, and I thought,

Chapter Fourteen

well, I won't go apply for anything else. I guess I'll stay home.

Then my whole home life changed so drastically, when my husband had the first stroke. He stayed down in the basement from then on, because he was paralyzed on his left side and couldn't get up and down the stairs. The basement had always been Paul's place, anyway. It was his shop, his refuge. He listened to his music and had all his favorite things close at hand.

Frank was so good to Paul. We converted the laundry room to a shower, with a curtain inside and the runoff going down the drain in the floor. Frank would move him in there with the wheelchair and help him bathe underneath that makeshift shower. He would get down on his hands and knees and wash Paul's feet. And if you said anything to him about it, Frank would just say, "That was nothing."

The second stroke came in about 2003. We were no longer able to care for Paul at home, so he went to live in a very nice nursing facility.

Just as was true throughout his life, everybody there just loved him. He had such a wonderful sense of humor and a lively mind.

With Paul being well cared for, I was free to travel to Germany, to see my sister. Frank's daughter, Linda, went with me in 2004.

Right away I could tell that Christel had changed tremendously. She was suffering the debilitating effects of Alzheimer's, and her disease was pretty far advanced. By her appearance you would never have guessed we were only four years apart. Looking at her,

I was struck by how my life in America had shielded me far better from the ravages of time. My life had been easier than hers.

When Christel saw me, she wrapped her arms around me and wept.

The Germans are not as loving or understanding as the American people. They can be very harsh, you know. If you don't understand something right away, they just say, "Oh, you are stupid!" So I knew she was under a lot of stress.

After her husband died, she still worked in the marketplace with her son, Hans, who had taken it over from my father. She did that until she no longer could help him or live on her own. Her youngest son, Paul, and his wife moved into the bottom floor of my sister's house so Christel could remain in her own home. She moved upstairs.

I'm so glad I got another chance to see her.

Christina (Christel) Velten Klein, born June 16, 1920 in *Köln* Germany, passed away seven years later, on March 13, 2011.

ᛨ

Paul died on August 9, 2007. He was eighty-nine.

The next day, the flag got hooked on the eagle's wing at the top of the flagpole. I couldn't see how I was going to get the flag down. The neighbors who live, now, in the house our son built years ago, offered to have their athletic daughter get it down.

I said, "Oh, no, no, no, no. I would not like her to take the risk!"

Chapter Fourteen

Gerda and Christel

Well, while I wasn't looking, she shimmied way up there and got the flag down. I have absolutely marvelous neighbors!

I love good music and, to this day, when I hear the music from *Tosca*, it brings back memories. Some sixty years after that beautiful night in Germany, when *Herr* Müller and I went to see *Tosca*, my neighbor called me and she said, "Gerda, I have tickets for the opera. Would you like to go with us?"

I said, "Oh I would like to! What is the opera about?"

She said, "*Tosca*."

I said, "I can't believe this!" It was like déjà vu, after all this time.

Because this neighbor of mine knew someone who worked at the theater, she had tickets for the most beautiful seats in the auditorium, in one of the boxes. I felt like, oh my, this is living! During intermission we were escorted to a special room for the VIPs! They served us hors d'oeuvres and champagne!

It was such a bittersweet evening. It couldn't have been a more different experience than my first viewing of *Tosca*, but when the lights dimmed and the curtain rose, I returned once more to that special evening in Germany and the memory of my first love.

☙

Frank was a big help to me after Paul died. We were a comfort to each other after the loss, which we both felt so deeply.

CHAPTER FOURTEEN

A couple of years ago, when Frank became ill, they told him he had maybe three months to live. Because he was going to need care, his daughters asked him where he wanted to go. He told them he wanted to come live with me, in this house.

His daughters were very attentive to Frank; they have been so supportive to me and were appreciative of the care I was happy to give to their father.

It was good for me, having his company full-time, although it wasn't easy to see him go downhill. He lived much longer than they predicted. I like to think it was because I took such good care of him.

Frank and Gerda

On the morning of April 6, 2014, I went to wake Frank for breakfast, as I usually did. I had called to him a couple of times already, but he hadn't made an appearance, so I approached him where he lay in his bed. As soon as I saw him, I knew he was gone.

Once, when I had been working particularly hard, and I was feeling a bit frazzled, I snapped at him, "Do you even love me?"

He made a show of thinking about it for a moment. Then, with the ghost of a smile, he said, "A little."

For his upcoming eighty-fifth birthday, which would have been on May 14, I'd bought him a card and written in it these words: "Even a little was enough for a lifetime." He died before I could give it to him.

Frank's memorial service was held in beautiful Adam's Chapel at the River View Cemetery in Portland, Oregon. I smiled through my tears when they played "My Way".

A few days later, I was on the porch when I noticed Sonny, the neighbor's dog, in the yard.

"Hi, Sonny!" I called.

He barked at me! He was looking everywhere for Frank.

When I did Frank's last laundry, I found in his pocket — dog biscuits, which he always carried with him. He was such a soft-hearted man!

When I look back over the course of my life, I see this thread that has always been Frank. When I was young, *Herr* Müller wasn't Frank, but it's like he was the foretelling of him. Who knows, if it weren't for *Herr* Müller, perhaps I would not have "recognized" Frank when I saw him.

Because of Frank, I gained a better understanding of what was missing between Paul and me. It shed a

Chapter Fourteen

whole new light on that awful chapter in our lives; the one that nearly ended our marriage.

Although I loved Paul very much, and we had a good life together, there was a room in my heart he never entered. It was a room I didn't even know existed until Frank found a home there — fitting effortlessly, like the last piece of a puzzle that just clicks into place.

Until you experience that kind of love, there are many other emotions that can wear the mask — admiration, respect and gratitude among them.

Meeting Paul at the end of the war, when I was exhausted by years of living with fear and deprivation, how could he not look like my knight in shining armor? Especially since he was not only handsome, but he possessed in abundance two qualities I greatly admire — intelligence and drive — and he offered me a whole new life, far from the detritus of war.

We did love each other, but I realize, now, that I was never really a good match for him. Whether he was consciously aware of it or not, Paul too must have felt that something was missing — he was looking for a room of his own, and I can hardly fault him for that.

I have been so fortunate to have had two wonderful men who played very different roles in my life.

I will never regret having loved them both.

About the Author

Terri Potts grew up in a small town in Southern Oregon. Although she majored in business and spent many years working in various aspects of the insurance industry, her real passions have always been writing, graphic design and family history.

In the course of researching her genealogy, with the intention of bringing her ancestors' stories to life for future generations, she became inspired to do something worth writing about in her own life. When her husband suggested a three-year adventure sailing down the Pacific coastline, through the Panama Canal and into the Caribbean aboard their forty-three-foot sloop, she swallowed hard and decided this was it!

That life-changing experience convinced her to chart a new professional course when she returned to the "real" world. Now, she brings together her talents for writing, photo restoration, graphic design and page layout to help others publish their stories, because family history is so much more than just names and dates.

Montage
BioGraphics

www.ingramcontent.com/pod-product-compliance
Lightning Source LLC
Chambersburg PA
CBHW070948180426
43194CB00041B/1724